HOW MIDSUMMER NIGHT

HOW MIDSUMMER NIGHT

A Memoir of Friendship and Loss

Janet Somerville

OPEN ROAD

INTEGRATED MEDIA
NEW YORK

Copyright © 2024 by Janet Somerville

ISBN: 978-1-5040-8935-7

Published in 2024 by Open Road Integrated Media, Inc.
180 Maiden Lane
New York, NY 10038
www.openroadmedia.com

This book is for the Holdsworths of Sunset House

In Memory of Richard
(May 26, 1950–November 28, 2007)

HOW MIDSUMMER NIGHT

How wrong, how right, how midsummer night

—Cole Porter, *High Society*

This above all, to thine own self be true.

—William Shakespeare, *Hamlet*

PROLOGUE

When my friend Richard was diagnosed at the age of 56—the age I am now—with glioblastoma, a rare and inoperable brain cancer, I decided to chronicle his journey, writing a long letter to him, capturing our conversations and reflecting on moments together that his wife and daughters hadn't necessarily shared, with the notion that I would give the piece to them as one version of his story.

What astonished me about his steady decline was Richard's choice to live his certain death with playfulness, graciousness and wit. If anyone had the right to wallow in self-pity and darkest melancholy, he did. But, remarkably, Richard chose the light: we all have a choice. And, although his luck in the cancer lottery was unacceptably bad, he was determined to show his family and friends that every waking moment is precious. Every day above ground is a good one.

At Richard's core he was essentially an entertainer. In spite of increased confusion about his daily reality, as the cancer spread at a gallop across his brain, he was able to retrieve vast swaths of information from his long-term memory and we nattered about literature (since he taught English and Drama for 25 years) and harvested musical show tunes to fit the moments we were inhabiting that were as much a part of both of us as the rhythmic excerpts from Shakespeare's canon or Oscar Wilde's clever aphorisms.

We are all worthy of our final moment and its telling, and it matters how we play it in the end.

ACT ONE

Diagnosis

The play's the thing.

—William Shakespeare, *Hamlet*

APRIL

Sunday April 15, 2007

Dear Richard,

Deb left a voicemail for me at home this afternoon that you had been taken to hospital unexpectedly, blood pressure wonky (maybe your recent prescription dose isn't quite right yet), and had trouble dressing yourself. I spoke with her directly moments ago and she said you exhibited stroke-like symptoms: garbled speech like British comic Rowan Atkinson as "Mr. Bean;" couldn't tie your tie in the favored double Windsor knot; couldn't loop the laces in your brogues or fasten the buttons on your shirt. Your fingers belonged to someone else.

And, I remember you telling me last week about driving the car off the road ten days ago and not knowing it until Deb asked you what the hell you were doing. That worried you and your blood pressure skyrocketed and you resolved to take the subway to work until you knew what was happening to you.

It took the EMS team minutes that seemed like hours to figure out which west end hospital would accept the ambulance and you're now at Trillium off the Queensway at Hurontario

Street in Mississauga. *Yehuppitsville* in Yiddish, meaning way the fuck out there. For any Torontonian north of Eglinton and west of Bathurst delineates the boonies.

Monday April 16, Evening

Deb says the blood marker indicates you haven't had a stroke, and that the potential diagnosis is far worse. She is exhausted, running on emotional empty as she keeps Alice and Heather moving through their paces of school life. Grade 12 at St. Clement's for Alice and Grade 7 at Kingsway College School for Heather. Alice has the distraction of her formal to look forward to on Friday night at the Design Exchange and hopes you'll be granted a day pass to get home to Sunset House to see her with her hair done in long loose waves, all tarted up for the night out with 20 of her closest friends and their dates. Heather is nearing the end of rehearsals for *Guys and Dolls* where she will be belting out the chorus parts in the eponymous song that you know so well from that perfectly crafted musical:

When you see a guy reach for stars in the sky
You can bet that he's doin' it for some doll

Maybe she's even one of Miss Adelaide's hot box dancers whisper singing *Take back your mink, take back your pearls, what made you think that I was one of those girls?* Maybe you'll get a day pass then to see her perform. One of the specialists on staff, though not the fellow assigned to your case, has a daughter in Heather's class at KCS and he's going to do what he can to make sure that you see her gadding about onstage. I'm pretty sure that you've used Damon Runyon stories with your AP Literature class in recent years because we took the boys to Stratford in 2005 to see

Cynthia Dale stomp about in the role of Salvation Army devotee Sarah Brown. Sheila McCarthy was a brilliant Miss Adelaide sniffling her way through the lament of being serially engaged to Nathan Detroit and never married:

> *... and, furthermore, just from stalling and stalling*
> *and stalling the wedding trip*
> *a person can develop la grippe ...*
> *from a lack of community property*
> *and a feeling she's getting too old*
> *a person can develop a bad, bad cold.*

We've both imagined ourselves Toronto's answer to Vivian Blaine, the Miss Adelaide of the original Broadway cast who gave Sinatra a run for his money in the film where Jean Simmons rang her bell for Brando's swoonworthy Sky Masterson.

Tuesday April 17

Deb tells me that they've found several tumors in the frontal lobe of your brain the size of those little jellybeans President Reagan kept on his desk in the Oval Office. As I type these words, I can't believe that this is happening to you. It is surreal and it's unacceptable. The tumors are inoperable and the search continues through a battery of unpleasant (banal use of litotes—rhetorical understatement so admired by literature teachers like us who are, inadvertently or not, compelled to preen their smartypants use of diction) tests, a perverse "*treasure hunt*" according to your oncologist Dr. H. He is baffled about the location of the primary cancer site, since brain cancer typically begins elsewhere and travels north on its way to the grave: your lungs are clear, your bowel is clear, your kidneys and liver are clear, your blood marrow is clean. A thorough battery of scopes and CAT scans comes up empty. Snake eyes.

You will tell the girls tonight about the cancer: an unthinkable conversation to be negotiated with your children.

Wednesday April 18

Now that Alice and Heather know about your brain cancer, Father D., our school chaplain, and I (as the in-house grief counselor) have started to parcel out this shocking news person-to-person at the Royal School.

I called Doug at home late last night to let him know directly before the word trickles out and gets passed around in a case of broken telephone at work. In his melancholic Celtic way he choked and swallowed and intoned in his quasi-Irish accent that smacks of St. John's, Newfoundland: "*It breaks me up. You know I love the guy.*" His current coping strategy that is equal parts hope and defiance is to keep you on the list for the choir tour to Spain at the end of June. "*Wot larks*" we three have had on tours past to England, Italy and Scotland with gaggles of trebles in tow.

Choir Tour, Scotland 2005

We're in Edinburgh on a rare night off, having tucked in our charges, the little 'uns in the choir, who have stashed their Gameboys under their pillows, at a recently renovated hotel in the "pubic triangle," a stone's throw from the strippers and the illustrious Fettes College, the elite private school for boys used by J.K. Rowling as the model for Hogwarts. The Grassmarket area below the castle is frequented by Ian Rankin's Detective Rebus and it is along these streets where we wander with Helen and Rob and Ian, following the "bunny trail."

Earlier in the evening after dinner we met the pre-nuptial hen party, including the mother of the bride-to-be, at the Blue Blazer pub, all kitted out in black fishnets, satin bodysuits, fluffy white press on tails and perky Playboy bunny ears sticking up from glossy jet headbands. All of them on the tear away from boyfriends, fiancés and husbands and delighted to meet some foreigners they could dupe for three pounds per "snog." All of you men ponied up your pound coins and enthusiastically, almost sacramentally, kissed the nubile blonde bride. And, here we are at midnight hopping behind the little tarts, teetering on their heels up to the entrance of Espionage, an underground hotspot that descends five stories below Edinburgh. The wooden stairs pulse with the 80s music (mostly Madonna and Tears for Fears) that spills up from the DJ's turntable as a few rainbow-wigged clowns wearing boxers stamped with pouting red lips stolen from Mick Jagger push their way past us up to the surface for the cooler night air.

This afternoon they tossed Frisbees and striped balls across the street weaving through the throng above Fleshmarket Close near St. Giles Cathedral where the choir sang evensong while the rest of Edinburgh celebrated Gay Pride Week. One of the clowns flirts with you by pinching your ass and you swivel your head back to me insisting, "if you all can't find me when you're ready to leave, don't come looking. I'll see you back at the hotel breakfast table."

Jolted from slumber in the wee hours I get a call from the overnight desk clerk telling me that one of the choristers has sleepwalked his way to a wedding reception on the ground floor. I retrieve the somnambulant darling unabashedly grooving in his underwear to the sounds of a local five-piece band blasting its way through the crowd-pleasing Village People hit YMCA. To the great amusement of the revelers, he bows his floppy head, willing to be returned to his room for the remaining few hours before the 6:30 wakeup call.

Thursday April 19

I've emailed our former colleague Gage, who two years ago was diagnosed with liver cancer and was essentially told to go home and prepare for the worst. To expect his own death. He refused. Opted for risky surgery by a cowboy of a cutter and now he is a newlywed and cancer free. You need to hear the hope of his story. A healing story against medical odds.

Mark has asked about you. Quietly inquires about updates. With his own mystifying heart trouble and experimental treatment Mark understands the bloom of fear and he knows loss having buried his first child, an infant son, as you'll remember.

You are "known and loved" by friends at work—it is not an empty-worded motto emblazoned on this year's mugs that Hal gave the faculty in August, filled with packages of jellybellies— the same size as the cancer bits embedded in your frontal lobe.

Your good news is the anti-inflammatories intended to reduce the swelling in your brain are working. Your oncologist explains that this a hopeful sign that the growths will be suitably responsive to radiation.

You left me a weepy and heart-crushing message on my work voicemail, Richard. Asking for a visit and for Doug and Father D. to come by your hospital room to offer communion, with those wafer-thin paper hosts that would be improved with a jar of Skippy peanut butter according to the boys who make the pilgrimage to the altar during school eucharists only for the sup of sickeningly sweet sacramental wine to boost them through the day. I've saved it in the ether just like my message at home from John Irving when I tried to convince him a year ago to participate in the Fall 2006 PEN Canada fundraiser at Convocation Hall with Nigerian Nobel Laureate Wole Soyinka and Azar Nafisi of *Reading Lolita in Tehran* fame. Like your message it has been saved and resaved. I will listen to you again when my eyes are not brimming with tears or the words "it's not fair" don't trip repeatedly across my lips. Not you, dear friend. This cannot be happening to you.

You, my fellow Gemini and birthday twin, who have been so kind and supportive in the decade that we've known each other. You, who have offered that shoulder to cry on: instinctively understanding my losses of my brother David who had turned twenty-five only weeks before I identified his body in a two-drawer morgue almost 14 years ago and of my sister's son Liam, stillborn before last Christmas. And, we wept together sitting in the wooden pew at the back of the school chapel as we read our student Alexander's piece about burying his parents within a year of each other when he was only twelve. A boy. And that achingly true phrase he wrote knowingly at seventeen: "*cancer is a broken heart.*"

Friday April 20

I saw Deb at your house this afternoon as I delivered tonight's meal, spaghetti Bolognese with crisp green salad and a crusty stick of French bread. The inimitable Catherine M., who you have said has "*the right mixture of compassion and intelligence and could run her own country,*" has organized fresh daily meals to be prepared by members of the extended Georgian community. The meals magically arrive and are left on the back porch for your three girls. A mundane and necessary task taken off Deb's plate. And, she's grateful and relieved to have nutritious food to serve your daughters when she is not equal to the task.

Today Father D. and I finished speaking directly to your classes. We're not quite Mickey and Judy organizing a mad-cap production out behind the barn, but we give it the old college try. The boys have been receptive faced with this shocking, unfathomable information. Asking real questions:

Did Mr. Holdsworth have any signs?

Is he in pain?

Do the doctors know how long ago the cancer started growing?

What can I do? Will he be OK?

Many of them have penned little *billet-doux* which we will take turns dropping by your house for Deb to bring along when she visits the hospital in the evening. Your favorite will be from Briande who wonders, "*how could there possibly be any room for a tumor in a mind as packed as yours, sir?*" I wanted to reassure them that you are yourself in your insistence that hospital food has been given a bad rap. That you aren't desperate enough to nibble on the tulip bulbs in the pots along the window ledge in your room. Not yet.

I think I'm still shrouded in shock as I tell and retell the narrative of this week. Though, I cried in one of my classes where we have been reading Dennis Bock's *The Ash Garden*. You know, the scene where Anton tenderly bathes his wife Sophie on the night he is obliged to provide her with the parting gift of her making: his promise to her to keep her company as she dies. No heroics. No ambulance. Simply bear witness. Mills burst into tears. Streaming down his face. All snotty like the scene Minghella scripted for Juliet Stevenson in *Truly, Madly, Deeply* and my heart cracked a little.

And, when other boys started asking questions, McMaster stepped forward bravely as the resident cancer expert. With the proper medical jargon, having lived the horror as his mother lay dying from metastasized ovarian cancer last February. He was so gracious. And comforting. Reminding others that doctors don't always know. In his mother's case she was told she would have a year, but she stretched that year into six. And, as she lived out her final days in palliative care at Princess Margaret Hospital, her family arranged for a special Valentine's Day visit with her horse. Triton traveled by trailer and Dierdre was wheeled by her children down to the semi-circular driveway where her chestnut-coated beauty unwittingly awaited his final crisp apple proffered by the outstretched hand of his mistress.

I wish you could have heard him. Witnessed his clear-eyed delivery. Your heart would have swelled ten-fold. Of course, to break the tension of such a grown-up moment, McMaster diverted his classmates' attention by announcing, *"they sell handcuffs for 8.99 at Kensington Market. Why wouldn't I buy four?"* Hunter added, *"I bought brass knuckles in Peru."* McMaster responded, *"That's jokes, bro. I want to go to Japan and learn to make Samurai swords."* And McCarthy quipped, in typical teenage boy *non sequitur, "That's rad. Don't breathe now. Smithyes just dropped his own atomic-bomb."*

Not a day goes by without such scatological appreciation. In my early days teaching adolescent boys I was perplexed by playful choruses of *"doorknob"* that echoed around the classroom at random, followed by barely suppressed giggles or comments like, *"that's gotta be Zimmerman; it smells like cottage cheese."* As usual, a well-placed fart cleared the air. As it always does during chapel services. Chaucerian, really, when you remember the fart like a thunderclap in "The Miller's Tale."

Later in the halls, one of your drama students little Haliday, approached me and said, those kind fawn eyes uplifted, *"You know how you can pay for healthcare to move up the line? I have a plan to raise money for Mr. Holdsworth so he can move to the front of the line. I think I can raise about eight thousand dollars."* And he means every cent of it. He also wants to tape improvised skits from his drama class and to burn a DVD to send to you as a distraction to complement the one from last year's production you directed of Sondheim's *A Funny Thing Happened on the Way to the Forum.*

A Funny Thing Happened on the Way to the Forum *Rehearsal, November 2006*

The campier the better is your guiding premise as you block out the scenes from Sondheim's musical that recently enjoyed rave reviews for its revival on Broadway starring Nathan Lane and his expressive eyebrows. It is Sondheim's political parody of pre-Christian Roman life that relies on physical comedy of farce and witty song lyrics to punch up the plot. Case in point: the trio of boys trilling,

> Everybody ought to have a maid
> Everybody ought to have a working girl,
> Everybody ought to have a lurking girl,
> To putter about the house.

The choreography has the three of them prancing and poncing their way through a soft-shoe routine, enthusiastically flicking feather dusters across each others' outstretched purple spandexed tushes, fluttering their false eyelashes à La Cage Aux Folles. And, loving every minute of it.

––––––

While Deb was picking up Heather from KCS, I chatted with Alice about university. She says she's most interested in the first year arts program at Carleton and they've offered her ten thousand in scholarship money over 4 years. Some of her St. Clement's friends are trying to convince her to go to Queen's because of its reputation. So I asked her if she really wanted to continue her education almost exclusively in the company of rich white kids and she said "*absolutely not*" but she was concerned that 80 at Carleton wasn't equal to 80 at Queen's or McGill. Not so. I told her about my friend Rajeev who did his undergrad at Carleton and went directly to a PhD in economics at Harvard and is now a full professor at Columbia in NYC. Her eyes lit up and she said "*I am so excited about university.*"

I asked Alice to show me her prom outfit tonight, which she happily trotted out. A fabulous sleeveless white dress that looks like it was designed for Aphrodite, cinched at the waist and billowy in the right places. Accessorized with adorable strappy gold sandals with chunky three-inch heels. I hope she gets photos taken when she's had her hair done, softly curled Greek goddess tresses. She'll be a knockout.

Saturday April 21

This morning you told me about you and Deb meeting with Peter, your lawyer friend from Trinity College days last night to update your will and to arrange for power of attorney. Both have been weighing heavily on your mind. That business is complete. Sobering, but necessary. It is a sensible task. One that our friend Wayson bullied me into completing on the eve of the quadruple bypass that saved his life.

You had the first MRI yesterday which you said felt like being in the Holland Tunnel while it was under construction. The banging and clanging so noisy, an arrhythmic clunk clank irritating in its unpredictability, as cacophonous and complicated as a Philip Glass composition. You got through it with an "*I don't care*" pill and by visualizing you and Deb lying naked on a

Moroccan beach when you first met. That image sustained you through the magnetic mapping of your brain that will allow the surgical team to figure out where exactly to have at you with their Black and Decker drill set. To get the tissue biopsy necessary to determine the radiation and chemo cocktail you will be prescribed. By the end of the procedure all of the vibration created unexpected foam like whipping cream that filled your mouth. Ever polite you asked the technician for a little crinkled paper cup in which to spit it out.

Father D. and Doug dropped by to offer you communion and you were grateful for their visit until the chaplain began fiddling with the fob of his pocket watch, checking the time over and over again. An insensitivity that baffles you, since he's someone whose business is pastoral care.

It's about 9:30 p.m. and I'm just home from visiting with you having not found you in 414, but moved to 211 in the neuro-surgery wing. Dr. H., your oncologist, has passed you off to the neurosurgeon Dr. Izakawa, whose name I continue to remember as Ishiguro, the novelist, because of his most recent and disturbing book *Never Let You Go.* In it he imagines a world wherein some humans are raised to be live organ donors who finally "complete" when they give up their hearts. In spite of your mnemonic device of Elmer Fudd saying "*Is a ca-wah on the side of the woad,*" it's a stretch for me. Izakawa. Iz-a-kawa. Then you're off chuckling to yourself as you recall the Looney Tunes Wagner parody when Fudd chants "*kill the wa-bitt, kill the wa-bitt*" as he continues his never-ending quest to pop off Bugs Bunny.

As you know I took Wayson out for a birthday lunch this afternoon, ambling distance from his house, to Central Perk in Riverdale. We were both compelled to scribble down the phrase on the chalkboard there attributed to novelist and poet Jim Harrison: "*The danger of civilization of course is that you'll piss away your life on nonsense.*" It's a good check. Wayson's sporting a ridiculous Hitler youth haircut that makes him look about 6 years old instead of his full 68. He's signed a first edition of his most recent novel *All That Matters* for you wishing you "*deep healing.*" I gave it to you tonight along with Scott Griffin's signed copy of *My Heart is Africa*, his memoir grounded in his abandonment of corporate life in Toronto that he exchanged for volunteer work flying small aircraft for Flying Doctors' Service in remote South African communities for two years. You are looking forward to both literary journeys as long as you don't drop the books as you're reading: page numbering confounds you as I discovered during an earlier visit when you were clearly frustrated by not being able to re-order your copy of *The Globe and Mail* that had slipped from your grip and slid across the floor.

Now that your legal affairs are in order—a revised will and power of attorney sorted—you seem to be less agitated and you're working up to writing each one of your girls a letter only to be opened after you die. Assuring Deb and Alice and Heather that they will endure without you. An unthinkable thought, but a sure kindness. Your worry from the outset—was that really only five days ago?—has been them. Not you. That is true grace.

Apparently, the first anti-depressant "*I don't cares*" they prescribed you made you feel schizophrenic. As we sat on a bench in front of the hospital entrance, you confessed that there is no filter for the voices inside or outside your head. Filipina cleaning ladies have been plotting a bridal shower and all you want to do is shriek at them, "*Choose the fucking green napkins already. Enough arguing.*" And, there's a little wombat snuffling around your legs. Unthreatening, of course. Even friendly, but mildly alarming in his persistent curiosity.

I brought you fresh berries tonight. Succulent blackberries the size of your thumb and plump organic blueberries with indigo skins, not quite that sweet taste of summer that Muskoka wild berries will be in July when I hope you'll be well into the radiation and chemotherapy cocktail the specialists will prescribe to try to extend your life once they have a pathology report in hand. Though, by then, everything may taste metallic, even your favorite hearty cabernet sauvignon.

My friend Dr. H. has chatted with Dr. R., the chief oncologist at Princess Margaret, to see about getting you a bed there for treatment. To make it a little easier on Deb and your daughters. He will call Deb directly. And, if anyone can make the arrangements, Dr. R.'s your man.

Sunday April 22

Doug called late this evening. In his cups a little. Or a lot. Choking back sobs about your whole situation and how you tried to assuage his fears when he phoned you. His melancholic Celtic temperament is crippling him. *No damned good*, as my Irish grandfather used to insist. Doug is trying to make sense of the diagnosis of inoperable brain cancer. But it makes no sense. It defies logic. Anyway you spin the narrative it is unacceptable. That you led a healthy lifestyle of good food, better wine, no smoking and regular exercise matters not a whit.

Monday April 23

Each time the twenty-third of April rolls around I marvel at the bard of Stratford-on-Avon who managed to be born and to die on this day; I refuse to believe it is the stuff of Shakespearean legend. The wheel does come full circle in our lives, more precisely for some than for others.

You, dear friend, left the most thoughtful message on my voicemail at work, paraphrasing that exquisite William Carlos Williams poem *"This is Just to Say"*. . .

that I have eaten the blueberries
which you were probably saving
for breakfast
forgive me
they were so sweet and so cold

And when I reached you this morning you answered the phone:
Dorothy? (your banker friend, I know)
We played along.
This isn't Kansas anymore.
It just hasn't been the same since the big storm took Toto out of town.

Then you rambled about Wayson's novel *All That Matters* that you intend to try to read post-biopsy to figure out *"if Poh Poh gets the lamborghini she's always wanted."*

The Imovane didn't work last night to settle you so you stayed up until sunrise, back pressed against the nursing station, long legs extended and crossed at the ankles, bare feet inside your Teva sandals writing your farewell letters. Instead of being depressed by the process, you are energized and hopeful. A heartwarming surprise to you. You daydream of hosting a summer dinner party with champagne glasses brimming in your magnificent century garden on Islington Avenue stretched behind Sunset House, which your parson grandfather built in kinder and gentler times.

You and Deb meet with your surgeon, Dr. M., this afternoon at 3:45. Deb has spent the past day reading *The Brain Tumor*

Book glossing over what matters in her understanding of your immediate future. She thinks she might even surf the Internet, which she couldn't possibly have done a week ago. It is astonishing how we adjust and figure out how to accommodate new realities when it is an issue of survival. Of one step at a time. Of breathing out and breathing in.

Tuesday April 24

There is no operating suite yet available for your neurosurgeon to schedule the biopsy. If he can bump someone else out, he might be able to work you in on the 30th. This waiting is untenable for Deb, though a little less so for you because in hospital, time has folded in on itself and it's difficult to keep track of the days that slip into one another. As if they are inside the wooden husks of Russian nesting dolls until all that remains is the air you breathe in and out. In and out.

We're calling in the school community connections at Princess Margaret Hospital and the chief oncologist there has been playing determined telephone tag with Deb. I always think of his son, who was diagnosed with leukemia in Grade 5, now a nursing student at McGill. How awful for his father to bear witness to his suffering and to have to hide his own. But his son's a survivor. Deb's making her Wednesday morning project to get in touch with another oncologist, Dr. W., whose quirky computer obsessed son we both taught, who has offered his consultancy services to see if your wait is typical or unacceptable, and if she should make a scene or have him intervene to get the attention you need.

You are considering your time at Trillium a social experiment and have already adapted to the bizarre rhythms of a hospital day and have lost track of the days of the week by your own admission. The nurses, the orderlies and the housekeeping staff provide you with endless amusement through their currently benign interaction with you. You are immersed in this new-to-you environment.

Back at school the boys forge ahead with absolutely no filter in their chatter as they settle down to work and I keep track of their witticisms to share with you especially if I anticipate the anecdotes will garner guffaws. On a grub day where school uniforms are optional, Briande arrives in a t-shirt with arrows pointing to each bicep emblazoned with "I don't need a permit for these guns" and announces:

"I'm pretty sure that there isn't any kind of flesh that I wouldn't try except human. I don't like pork, though, because pigs are so smart."

"I actually ate guinea pig in Ecuador; it's too salty," chirps Louis.

"What about dog?" Pauper asks.

"I'd be weirded out, but I'd try it."

A little later Sifton says, *"I'm taking my golden retriever Henley on Megan's Walk. He'll probably charge some kid in a wheelchair. Therapy dog, my ass."* And on it goes.

With the rain last night and the sun all day today the carpet of daffodils is radiant along the north stone wall of your driveway at 1398 Islington. I hope you'll be able to see those lush harbingers of Spring. Doug wants to know if he can transplant the deep purple irises you gave him and Diane for their garden because where they are currently they grow strong straight stalks but do not bloom. Or, does he have to wait until fall? You are our gardening guru. We are both hopeless horticultural wannabees.

Your Alice received her final offer of admission today from University of Toronto which means she's batting a thousand.

She's leaning towards arts at Carleton University in Ottawa, but Deb confessed to me that she might need Alice close to home in the fall, so Alice is going to visit the Trinity campus, your *alma mater*, as well as the University of Guelph, only an hour away by car, to try to decide between those.

Wednesday April 25

Keith is fretting about you constantly. This morning he confided that you have entered his dreamscape. And he rarely dreams. Last night he found himself sitting in a stadium beside your girls and they told him to address his concerns to you directly. And then you appeared, conjured Big Brother style, your face filling the Jumbotron at the Rogers Centre, like Liza Minelli's did in the early 80s at the concert when Frank Sinatra forgot the words to his signature song, *My Way*. But Keith can't remember what you said. No doubt you crooned, mimicking Old Blue Eyes, *"Now, the end is near, it's time to face the final curtain."*

I drove to sleepy little Ancaster this afternoon for my uncle's funeral. Mostly to hug my cousins, his sons, of whom I am fond. I was twitchy throughout the service because of the dearth of music and now I want to consider what music I'd like at my own funeral. Something liturgical and not a dirge. Something unexpected like "O Thou the Central Orb" with those chest thumping chords and that gorgeous descant for treble voices— the Florentine triumph you'll remember from that Italian Choir Tour in 2001. Outside one of the churches you snipped a pale peach magnolia blossom, smuggled it back to Canada in a wet sock in your suitcase and bullied it into growing in Toronto where it was naturally out of its element. We got caught in a massive downpour near the Trevi Fountain and bought collapsible umbrellas for 3000 Lire—the equivalent of four Canadian dollars. I still have mine. Deep green and a little worse for wear, having blown inside out more than a few times. I'd also want Ella Fitzgerald singing Cole Porter's *"I Get a Kick out of You"* because it's playfully morbid and I am a resolute musical theatre slut, as you know:

> *My story is much too sad to be told*
> *but practically everything*
> *leaves me totally cold.*
> *The only exception I know is the case*
> *when I'm out on a quiet spree*
> *fighting vainly the old ennui*
> *and I suddenly turn and see*
> *your fabulous face.*

It's not upsetting to contemplate the score of my own funeral and I can tell you because you won't be creeped out. It's a pragmatic decision.

Gage phoned me tonight. Rambling in his ebullient Gageness how much he was touched by his visit with you in hospital. How he believes your positive attitude will make the critical difference once you begin your chemo cocktail.

Deb says she's had a long-time deal with you re: parenting—that she would carry those babies for the requisite nine months, endure labor (which you told me as a spectator seemed that her pain was akin to having a car door slammed on her hand over and over again), give birth and you would take care of the next twenty years. You heartily agreed, but you still owe her seven more years by her reckoning as Heather is only thirteen.

Doug stomped through the school kitchen where I was chatting with Jeanne and greeted us in his best Lionel Barrymore impersonation with *"how now, you black and midnight hags."*

You can picture it. Perhaps even like a bumbling and stumbling Peter O'Toole in *My Favorite Year*. Jeanne has covered the scope of spiritual tokens and got you a St. Jude medal (lapsed Catholic that she is) and healing stones from a store on the Danforth called The Good Earth, after the beloved Pearl Buck novel. She's instructed me to tell Deb to soak the stones in the sea salt to purify them for your healing use. She really is a peach.

Friday April 27

This morning you told me about interpreting what is happening in terms of a Bergman film. The dice have been rolled and the camera pans in on one cupped hand. Waiting for the roll to be revealed. Boxcars? A pair of sixes? No. The dreaded snake eyes: those matching single dots.

By your own admission you've been "*sleeping on a mattress of prayers.*"

Sunday April 29

You have a beautiful spring day to be home for several hours. Hours of reprieve spent exclusively in the company of your girls before the biopsy scheduled for noon tomorrow. The neurologist, Dr. M., is content that the anti-seizure medication has stabilized you for now. That you won't fall on your face, as Buster Keaton might have gamboled in *The Cameraman*.

When we chatted on Friday you were relieved that you could share a meal at home, though Heather refuses to talk. Has shut down. Like you, she's normally a verbal maniac. Loquacious. Articulating her recent silence you choked back your tears. Now that you are back at the house your memory of leaving the girls sitting on the well-worn stairs in the front hall passively, helplessly as you were wheeled past them on a stretcher and loaded into the ambulance, can be replaced. You can stop fretting about that lasting image indelible as a tattoo.

Monday April 30

You left the most delightful forward-looking message on my school voicemail this morning at 9:08 a.m. before you were prepped for the procedure which you confide is risky: "*a sneeze and a slip of the surgeon's scalpel and I could be Daniel Day Lewis in My Left Foot.*" I've seen you play at Christy Brown in manic moments where you've gloried in the notion that he was reputed to have had "*the most active left foot in all of Ireland.*"

There is a bottle of *Veuve Cliquot*—that old widow—hidden in the basement waiting for a summer feast in your yard. We'll sing then with our champagne flutes raised to the star-peppered sky, toasting your reclaimed health and Cole Porter's wit:

> *Have you heard? It's almost dawn.*
> *Mow the bubbly and pour the lawn.*
> *Well, did you evah?*
> *What a swell party it is!*

I've been watching the clock and was twitchy during the national anthem in the St. Alban's Chapel, swatting hands out of pockets as those overindulged boys slouch and grumble their way through *O Canada, our home and native land* (so cleverly and scathingly parodied by A.A. Gabriel in Thomas King's *Green Grass Running Water* as, *Hosanna-da, our home on native's land*). Father D. asked the assembled mass to send positive energy your way especially at noon.

At noon I'll be meeting with my Writer's Craft class wherein last period Schwartz announced that he was fresh from a command performance with the Dean of Students, an anticipated meeting about his serial lateness:

"I had the weirdest encounter just now. I felt like Mr. James was hitting on me. He reached down and jangled his keys up and down, up and down and it looked like he was masturbating. More of a flirtation I thought. Maybe I'll pen My Secret Life, *a sequel to my bestselling breakout memoir* Sleeping with the Headmistress."

He was bemused and unthreatened, just like Dakin in Alan Bennett's *The History Boys*, defiantly chirping *"I'm black and blue"* from imagined assaults.

You've been assured that you will be spared the bolts of a metal halo being screwed into your skull as the neurosurgeon navigates his way through a bored hole to snip tiny pieces of the tumor which I imagine has outstretched tentacles the length of my piano-playing fingers burrowing deeper by the day into your brain.

It's 4:30 and I'm just off the phone with your Alice who says you are in the recovery room and allegedly conversing appropriately with the critical care nursing staff, having been woken up from the general anesthetic and had the breathing tube removed without incident. Deb hasn't seen you yet but will be sure to do so before she returns home to retrieve your daughters for a visit.

7:00 p.m.

I'm waiting down at the Enwave Theatre at Harborfront, having moments ago run into publisher Louise Dennys with her world-famous author Ian McEwan in tow. Just the two of them, so, of course, the impeccably mannered Louise introduced me to the man who's next-to-last book *Saturday* was about a neurologist. I can't remember if you've already read it, and if you haven't, you will. McEwan shadowed one of London's top neurosurgeons for about two years. He's here tonight to read from *On Chesil Beach*, the new novel about a sexually dysfunctional couple on their wedding night in the early sixties. An evening which goes predictably awry.

Before I left the Q and A that followed McEwan's delightful interview, he drew attention to the complete absorption he witnessed daily in the work of the neurosurgeon he shadowed. That essential and energizing dissolution of self. The focus on the work excluding all else: McEwan's version of working happiness that occasionally consumes him as he writes. Rare and joyful.

We've both felt that way when a class has gone unexpectedly well, like the time I had the boys listen to Glenn Gould's distinct recordings of Bach's Goldberg Variations as background to our reading of David Young's play *Glenn* and one of the boys observed that in the second version it seemed to him that "*the pauses in between mattered as much as the notes themselves. You can tell that the pianist has lived his life and understands the resonance of silence.*" Imagine being sixteen and having that kind of insight!

When you were sixteen you posed for the black and white glamor photo shots that landed you those beer ad contracts. When you were sixteen, I was learning to walk, to toddle about on my own two feet. When I was sixteen, I played Mrs. Paroo in *The Music Man* offering such conventional romantic wisdom in a contrived Irish brogue I'd copied from my own grandfather: *If you keep the flint in one drawer and the steel in the other, you won't strike much of a fire.* Or chastising Marian about keeping her crush on Harold Hill to herself: *Will you ever tell him? Won't you ever tell him? Ah, yes? Ah, no. Ah, fiddlesticks! Just open your mouth and let it come out.*

MAY

Tuesday May 1

Deb wrote that the surgeon removed fluid from your brain as he was biopsying the tissue. Reduced the pressure building there. You are still resting in the critical care unit and permitted fluids by mouth, though your appetite is ravenous due to the steroids pumping through you to manage the swelling. All part of a new normal when MDs have at your head with a drill bit.

You'll remember me telling you about my visit to the lock down psychiatric unit at Toronto General when I went to see my friend JJ. It was *One Flew Over the Cuckoo's Nest* redux. There were three Nurse Ratchets in the plexiglass booth that separated them from the five patients in their so-called care of benevolent neglect, one of whom was my cherished friend. His anti-psychotic meds had been stolen a month previously from his checked luggage on board a flight from Florence to Paris, where he found himself going cold turkey, inadvertently fucking with his delicately balanced brain chemistry.

There was a young woman in the unit tethered to a bed with canvas restraints, who had tried to kill herself with a power drill bit to her temple and a twenty-something man who bowled with his own shit and JJ quipped with extraordinary insight and candor, *"Somerville, how can I compete with that? I know when to fold."*

You and I roared at his quick wit and were touched by his generosity. Oscar Wilde was right: *In life, we are all in the gutter. Some of us just tend to look up at the stars.* Like you, JJ is a star gazer.

The woman hired to take on your Literature and Drama classes for May is a fresh-faced, pixie-haired, natural blonde with a French manicure and she's a certified Geography teacher. As Jeanne snarked, "*I wonder who her uncle is.*" Your students are unwilling to accept that she is a replacement for you, just as they were wary of me when I covered a few of your classes in the early days of your absence. I certainly don't expect her to leap across the hall, throw open the door to my classroom, lunge into Room 104, and exclaim *non sequitur,* "*In a handbag?*" How many times in recent years have you channeled a Lady Bracknell in *The Importance of Being Earnest* to rival Dame Judi Dench, leaving me smiling broadly and the boys in my class bemused, if not entirely perplexed?

You'll remember the time when novelist Michael Winter came to my Canadian Literature class to read from his novel *The Big Why.* Michael likes to walk the razor's edge and selected an excerpt about his randy 19th century protagonist, artist Rockwell Kent, who, commenting on his sexcapades, notes that there's "*nothing quite as lovely as a woman's tongue on your asshole.*" But Kent's sentiment wasn't the showstopper. While many of the boys chuckled, Douglas, sitting beside me at the horseshoe-shaped table, tried unsuccessfully to whisper in his gravelly voice, "*Ma'am, tell me what could be lovelier than that?*" His hypothetical question slash comment sent Michael to the floor gleefully collapsing in hysterics, trumped at his own game.

Heather has made a little shrine at home of religious/spiritual artifacts including the healing stones Jeanne sent you along with the St. Jude medal. I'm thinking he's the patron saint of lost causes. Didn't Danny Thomas name a hospital after him? And, if so, why is that trivia lodged in my long-term memory? Can I dump it now to make room for something lasting?

Wednesday May 2

Giles was here at the Royal School to play the organ during the confirmation service presided over by the Bishop of Toronto, so I had lunch with him and Doug at Pauper's Pub, where the longtime barkeep Patrick took care of our mid-day whims. Giles wants to visit you and reminded us that he's known you longer than anyone other than your sister Elizabeth. Probably 45 years— since you were little Chip Holdsworth singing as a treble, and often the descant lines, at St. Simon's on the curve of Bloor Street before it crosses the viaduct and turns into the Danforth.

Thursday May 3

You've been discharged to enjoy the next stretch of days at home in the glorious garden while you wait for the pathology report that will wend its way to you next week. The judgment.

Friday May 4

I've come from reveling with you and Deb for about an hour with the late afternoon sun dappling the new blades of Spring grass, filtered through the bursting little leaves of the mature trees. The ground is plush carpet soft and warm under bare feet.

Today a burst of orange tulips catches your eye, looking almost like trilliums in their triangular petalled form. The early periwinkle cilla is up, creating a creeping carpet between the pale yellow daffodils. I know so little about flowers and nurturing them, while you have made a studious habit of it with those glorious beds that line about 400 feet of your property reaching out to the manicured lawn of the golf course. The poppy leaves are lush, but the papery blooms won't present themselves until July with their blueblack stamen and vermillion petals the size of a mug of *café au lait*.

You offer to nurture a cutting from your burgeoning lavender Rose of Sharon and prepare it for me to transplant into my own perennial bed later in the season.

Remarkably you are not yet angry. At a god or the fates who've woven the wrong pattern under the tree of knowledge that is your particular life. You are not inclined to rage on the heath like Shakespeare's Lear. Olivier was the definitive old king anyway. No "*blow winds, crack your cheeks, rage . . . blow*" for you. Not yet. You've got the loyal servant Kent's attitude anyway, who "*hates him that would upon the rack of this tough world stretch him out longer.*" You'd hoped to be teetering around in your nineties, diaper bound, muttering your own peculiar brand of purple nonsense, singing in a parody of Piaf, "*je ne vinaigrette rien*" or anyone of the chirpy tunes from the revisionist Rogers and Hammerstein classic *The Sound of Mucus,* but no such indignity is in store. You're sure of that.

It is unacceptable at 56 to be facing death, but you are. You say that you've been told that the pathology report will reveal varying degrees of bad. It seems incongruous and unthinkable as I sit across from you in a lawn chair sharing a pot of Earl Grey tea. The stitches and staples of the incision on your head behind your right ear look like a zipper and I know that through that portal the neurosurgeon put a drill bit to your skull to biopsy the nasty tissue which you have been told is advanced and inoperable brain cancer.

Your lack of anger is a gift to your family. Deb is angry enough for you all and so she should be. She will be left here. Behind. While you, blithe spirit, journey on.

Each day you wake as yourself you are grateful. Grateful that the anti-seizure medication and the steroid infused anti-inflammatory are working and allowing you a distinct clarity of thought, articulation and appreciation of the moments left in this only life. You savor the rich Kenyan blend of coffee beans ground each morning and appreciate quiet moments alone with classical music selections on CBC Radio Two for company after Alice and Heather head off to school.

Monday May 7

You and Deb hoped to see the Emily Carr exhibit today, because her recent reading of Susan Vreeland's *The Forest Lover* has rekindled her passion for Carr's vibrant landscape paintings, but, of course, the Art Gallery of Ontario is closed being Monday. A dark day for galleries. You both got your summer haircuts instead. A swath left long on top of your head to flop over the patch where the incision is.

On the weekend you took the family out for a fabulous meal at Merlot, a little French restaurant on Bloor. About half a mile as the crow flies from your place. Heather surprised you all by not only ordering but also enjoying venison. She didn't find it gamey at all. Alice had shrimp pasta that she pushed about her plate. Deb says she could get used to such occasions especially since the bill isn't sky high *sans bouteilles de vin*. She is content to sip a glass of a hearty red along with her meal. *Ça suffit.* It must be enough now that she's always the designated driver.

You will never find yourself behind the steering wheel again. The last time you drove at the beginning of April you were surprised to be inexplicably swerving into the oncoming traffic on Royal York Road. Your neurologist explained that you were probably experiencing a seizure induced from the pressure of your then unknown tumors. In our climate conscious world, you are content to have your driving days behind you and to no longer be contributing to the carbon footprint.

Deb's sister Ginny has offered to come and stay for awhile—make the long journey from New Zealand where they grew up—and she is the only person Deb would consider adding to the four of you. But she doesn't need her here yet. Would rather be the four of you. For now.

Heather is acting out. Her upset amplified by the hormonal upheaval of adolescence. In her teenish way she finds it "*way too depressing*" to come home to the tumor talk where symbolically the whole family has cancer. Heather would rather be at Sherway Gardens watching a film with her friends, one of those saccharine summer blockbusters with sophomoric humor and little else, like *Blades of Glory*, or *The Spy Who Shagged Me*.

Tuesday May 8

The folks at Trillium sent Deb home with a contraption to remove the staples suturing your incision and you've got an early morning appointment with your GP tomorrow to have them yanked. You're both expected at the hospital on Thursday to hear what the pathology report reveals. You are not holding your breath and anticipate the news will be bad or very bad, and you plan to keep it to yourselves and parcel it out to your daughters on a need-to-know basis. It is nobody else's business.

Wednesday May 9

Sifton found me in the halls to ask, "*Is there any new word on Mr. H.?*" When I told him you would likely receive the biopsy results today, he closed his eyes and crossed his fingers on both hands behind his back. He has just finished his own chemo treatments for a benign brain tumor that was removed in January. It wore him down, but he's his perky elfin self now. Uncomplaining and hopeful in spite of his daily exhaustion. Then he told me, "*I'm going to have to get braces for six months and I'm going to ask them to tighten the wires until I cry to make it go faster.*" His orthodontic plan fought with shouts of "*sphincter*" and "*anus*" as the Grade Elevens crammed for a bio test on the digestive tract enthusiastically barking out the terms to elicit the heartiest laugh along the corridor.

When I got to your place this afternoon to deliver your laptop and a few more messages, both you and Deb were snoozing in the garden chairs. Deb in a Zen pose, cross-legged, head thrown back facing the sun, arms extended on the rests. Looking absolutely serene. Both of you grubby from weeding the perennial beds. I waited for you to stir, not wanting to interfere with the restful rising and falling rhythms of the alpha waves in your chests.

You had the staples removed by Dr. McD. this morning and now there is an angry looking ridge of scar tissue, though you say there's no pain. But, you complain it's itchy where hair is sprouting through the shaved patch.

Whatever is disclosed by the hospital team now managing your care, you will keep it between you and Deb: to protect Alice and Heather, but not to lie to them either. You have been cautioned from the outset about the gravity of your condition, though you are not "*a grave man*" like Mercutio in *Romeo and Juliet*, yet you are regrettably and admittedly "*fortune's fool.*"

ACT TWO

Treatment

See how life bends us . . . until we become entirely who we are.
—Timothy Findley, *Elizabeth Rex*

Thursday May 17

You were fitted for your radiation mask today and say you felt like Gumby, that 1960s green plasticine figure, easily bent out of shape. You seem fascinated by the process, almost as if you're having a costume designed by one of the Stratford crew for a production of *Oedipus Rex*. Do you remember when we took the boys to see that awful production with all of the characters in platform shoes, gold *lamé* jumpsuits and oversized headgear? Burke got tossed out because he started to do a striptease—out of fork-in-your-eye boredom—in front of one of the snoozing seniors at the back of the orchestra section. At least he didn't fold his program like an airplane and light on fire before launching it towards the stage. If only Sophocles had had the foresight to anticipate the need for comic relief *where a chap kills his father and causes lots of bother*, to quote Irving Berlin—a need greater than the one to sympathize with suffering.

You tell me you've been covered in a substance akin to raw pizza dough to make the mold and it has been pressed down around your neck and shoulders and it seems like you've become another species, adapting to your environment and able to breathe through your ears. The procedure takes about two hours as time bends in on itself. And you can't help but think of *Mask*, starring Cher as the distraught and loving mother of a son who has bone cancer and his face hardens. Not worried that your face will do the same, but rather acutely aware of other suffering made manifest in the movie.

The technician and your radiologist have walked you through the process that you will endure every day for six weeks. The regime begins with an early morning routine of ingesting chemo pills the size of milkbone dog biscuits. Whatever cocktail you've been prescribed is intended to make the brain tumors more receptive to the radiation blasts. At this stage you are choosing to be fascinated by the light show that happens thanks to the 3D map of your brain and the location of the stage four cancer. Nylon mesh secures you into position as laser beams are guided through the portals in your mask and you are baked through an MRI in a matter of minutes: something off the soundstage of a Lucas film or the set of *Star Trek: The Next Generation*. If only you could find yourself on the HoloDeck being entertained by flawless and seductive holograms of Marlene Dietrich, Catherine Deneuve or Sophia Loren, whisper-singing their way through, *"I'm wild again, beguiled again, a whimpering simpering child again. Bewitched, bothered and bewildered, am I."*

JUNE

Wednesday June 13

Today is graduation at the Royal School and your Alice graduates tomorrow from St. Clement's. She has had a pre-grad workshop on how to sit like a lady. Knees together. Legs crossed tidily and firmly at the ankles. So primly 1950s. She thinks it's completely ridiculous.

We are presenting the inaugural Richard Holdsworth/ Tarragon Theatre fellowship tonight at RSGC to Carra. Susan Coyne, Tarragon Theatre's playwright-in-residence, has been instrumental in helping me set up the experience. Since Carra is interested in the production end of things, he will shadow the blocking of Morris Panych's *Benevolence*, a world premiere that Panych will direct to open the 2007-2008 season. He'll also get to spend a day with Richard Rose, the artistic director about whose work you have been unwaveringly enthusiastic for years at Tarragon, at Canadian Stage, and at the Stratford Festival.

Susan has put a package together for you of seasons one (*Hamlet*) and two (*Macbeth*) of *Slings & Arrows*, the show she co-writes with Bob Martin and Mark McKinney, set among a fictional theatre troupe called the New Burbage Company. You will enjoy the playfulness of the series wherein each season's production problems mirror the Shakespearean play the company is performing. And you'll get a kick out of other school parents featured, including swish elegant Paul Gross as a talented director reclaiming himself after a breakdown and his real-life spouse Martha Burns as a diva playing Gertrude, an on-screen antithesis of her sweet, thoughtful, affable self. Many other Stratford Festival actors whose faces will be familiar to you from your years in the audience star or have essential supporting roles: Steven Ouimette, Colm Feore and William Hutt. There are charming guest star turns from Sarah Polley, Rachel McAdams and Luke Kirby, too.

Deb's sister Ginny is here for about 10 days and the two of them chatter like schoolgirls. Burbling happily in their own peculiar syntax in your back garden, sipping generous glasses of chilled Chardonnay. It is the first time I've seen Deb relax since your diagnosis. And, it's obvious from your banter that you are also fond of Ginny, who has flown from New Zealand to buoy the clan with her kindness and wit. It is reassuring to Deb that Ginny is a psychotherapist capable of assessing and managing your collective mental health.

Saturday June 30

I've been away in Spain on the school choir tour which you would have joined had you not been felled by this heinous disease. I managed to send you a couple of postcards from Montserrat and Madrid and Toledo where we were offered up a vision of the Holy Grail—which didn't look like the cup of a carpenter to me. Irreverent that I am I immediately think of the *Monty Python* sketch with the hollowed coconuts used as the sound effect for clattering horse hooves, recently revived in productions of *Spamalot*: where you can surely hum along to:

> *Life's a piece of shit, when you look at it.*
> *Life's a laugh and death's a joke, it's true.*

While the choir was warbling in Spanish cathedrals, I returned to the news that you were hospitalized with pneumonia. Well, *merde* and *merde encore une fois*. Just what you didn't need. But I suppose it's not that much of a surprise because your immune system has been blasted to the stratosphere. Little ions of Richard spreading their goodwill way above ground; a literal out-of-body experience. *Fairies away!*

A Midsummer Night's Dream, *November 2004*

You have your own fairies to direct in Shakespeare's comedy. None of the boys or girls flinch at flitting about with diaphanous wings firmly anchored between their shoulder blades, or having their faces painted with green and gold glitter, vines trailing down their necks and under their sequined costumes for this caper play-within-a-play plot where anything goes in the Forest of Arden. There Bottom turns into an ass, a verbal and visual pun, and the lovers Demetrius, Lysander, Helena and Hermia fall under Puck's mischievous love potion spell.

The prettiest boys are cast as Puck and his master, the fairy king Oberon, dressed in shimmering body hugging fabrics and tights pulled by the two of us from the Stratford Costume Shop and the girls, all from our sister school Havergal College. Though lovely enough in their own painted fashion, the girls are almost an afterthought, aside from the fairy queen Titania who is given some of the best lines and is played with chutzpah by a British student here on exchange.

You've decided to choreograph the curtain calls as a traditional Renaissance dance that involves stomping and clapping after Puck delivers his grand apology that enraptures the audience each night:

If we shadows have offended
Think but this and all is mended
That you have but slumbered here
While these visions did appear
And this weak and idle theme
No more yielding but a dream.

JULY

Tuesday July 3

In our conversation tonight you explained that during your ten-day-long convalescence at Toronto General that in addition to being given respite from your daily radiation/chemo cocktail at Princess Margaret that you endured another barbaric procedure: having your lungs vacuumed. To remove fluid and blood clots. Another enemy holding your body at siege: pulmonary embolism. You are expanding my vocabulary more successfully than the antiquated and pedantic *Words Are Important*.

That hospital stay wore you down. Down to a nub. Ready to toss in the towel. At the outset you were willing to sign on to the experimental dosages of radiation and chemo, if the discomfort would afford you extended quality time with Deb and the girls. You are hoping to be granted this summer with them, but you are not sure you will live through it. Each time you walk with me along the garden, you become wistful about the flowers, many of which you suspect you have seen bloom for the last time.

Yet, just as we're both on the brink of tears you launch into an enthusiastic Ethel Merman falsetto of "*Ev-ery thing's com-ing up ro-ses and daf-fo-dils. Ev-ery thing's com-ing up spring-time and prair-ie flowers*" and release us from our maudlin moment.

Monday July 16

Your girls are away at camp, so you and Deb are planning to have your own change of scenery up at Pat and Mike's cottage.

I've been speaking with Alannah Campbell to try to set up a Sound Portrait for you *en famille*. She and her fellow CBC colleague Judy Maddren embarked on this lovely business recently and have been facilitating memorable interviews and creating audio collages for posterity.

Deb wants you to talk about the history of Sunset House since she has no one else to ask and figured that this portrait would be a good little project for you all. Alannah pays homage to George Bernard Shaw on her website, insisting, "*If you cannot get rid of the family skeleton, you may as well make it dance.*" You'll have yours contorting in an Argentine tango. And, you'll enjoy spending time with Alannah, as you did having her son in your Grade 10 class; they are both playful wits and "*smarter than your average bear.*" She will have you spilling secrets you didn't even know you were keeping from yourself.

Thursday July 26

You left me a delightful invitation to join you and Deb in the glorious garden for a glass of wine this evening and I can't return the call because it's too late. I hope Doug was able to drop by. I'm looking forward to our Monday morning *répas* of coffee and croissants, though admittedly anxious about witnessing your physical decline.

I know, because you've told me, that you've been stumbling and falling. A lot. "*I'm not steady on my pins and I'm sporting the skinned knees of a six-year-old learning to ride a bicycle without the training wheels.*" And now you have your own version of those supports to extend your independence: a light-weight aluminum walker, common among the nursing home blue rinse set. Susan Stroman used them to great comic effect in her choreography for Mel Brooks's musical *The*

Producers in the scene where Max Bialystock woos the old ladies to raise the money to produce *Springtime for Hitler*—the worst play ever written. Especially funny is the segment where Stroman parodies the infamous Rockette tin soldier routine, as the identically costumed old broads wearing blue-rinse-permed wigs, both male and female dancers, collapse in a row, walker upon walker, along the west side of Central Park. *"That's soooo clever,"* you beamed after you finally saw the film.

You've also lost about 40 pounds. The extra fifteen you've been trying to shed from Christmas 1995 long gone. Most of the weight fell away during your final weeks of treatment when you couldn't even stomach sips of water without vomiting: the ultimate discouragement as you soldier on. Dehydration and the utter exhaustion made you crazy with frustration, and unable to move from your hospital bed nestled under the back window in your living room with its garden view of riotous bloom.

Monday July 30

I expected to find you a whisper of yourself and was relieved to see you still in your face, tanned from being in the garden, which is beginning to produce its herb and vegetable bounty of coriander, cilantro, basil, tomatoes, dill, cucumber, and onion. Your legs are sticks and scabbed from the recent falls because of your left deficit. You've put your own spin on that numbing sensation that presents like a stroke symptom, wondering one morning who was grabbing your balls so enthusiastically soon to realize that the strange hand was actually your own.

An occupational therapist was bathing you and helping you dress when I arrived so I got the croissants and homemade jams—strawberry, quince and currant—spread out on the long table draped in the lemon and indigo Provençale print cloth in the backyard.

The hospital bed set up in your living room has a *cirque du soleil* pole running from floor to ceiling so you can leverage yourself in and out of bed with your stronger right side. The sinister side shot. I tease you that we could film a parody pole dancing routine to post on YouTube and the idea appeals to your playfulness and enthusiasm to be self-deprecating. Can't you just imagine inviting your internet audience to join you? Afterall, you could belt in your best Liza Minnelli impression,

What good is sitting alone in your room?
Come hear the music play.
Life is a ca-ba-ret, old chum.
Come to the ca-ba-ret.

A nurse came around 11:30 to inject the anti-coagulant, which you now receive twice daily. Post chemo and radiation you are at risk for accumulating blood clots and the memory of having had your lungs vacuumed is all too fresh and terrifying to contemplate enduring ever again.

The anti-inflammatory pills you're on to prevent the brain tumors from swelling have you revved up. I can barely keep up with your chatter. Not that I ever could. Today you were remembering being a boy, maybe twelve, hauling an old victrola around Manotick organizing a performance of the neighborhood kids in *A Midsummer Night's Dream*—introducing the locals to the rhythm and rhyme of Shakespeare's language that you appreciated even then.

Set your heart at rest, the fairyland buys not the child of me from Titania's speech about the Indian boy or Puck's closing words thought to be the bard's own apology and a shameless appeal for applause. And, you've always been shameless about courting applause:

Give me your hands, if we be friends
And Robin shall restore amends.

Your life is a walking shadow. Yet. Fretting its hour upon the stage.

You've envisioned the spreading cancer as the gooey villain Pizza the Hutt in *Spaceballs*, amorphous primordial ooze with personality. A waking dream had the top of your skull flipping open painlessly and the evil body snatcher scuttling away like those "ragged claws" in T.S. Eliot's "The Love Song of J. Alfred Prufrock." If I could will it, I would—that your diagnosis and treatment are just a big stupid medical mistake. And I imagine that you'd have the *chutzpah* to be gracious about its inconvenience and worry. No hard feelings. An exaggerated French shrug. Really.

When you're too agitated to sleep you get up and polish the silverware. Thinking you're being helpful in spite of the three a.m. clanking of cleaning cutlery, that has the rest of your family startling awake and worried about an imagined intruder in the house.

Tuesday July 31

Wayson and I went to see Saroyan's beautiful play *The Time of Your Life* at Soulpepper Theatre this afternoon, thoughtfully directed by Albert Schultz. The premise would suit you. I've written down the preface to the play because it reminded me of the attitude you've adopted in the face of a bleak and limited future:

In the time of your life, live—so that in that wondrous time you shall not add to the misery and sorrow of the world, but shall smile at the infinite delight and mystery of it.

Any one life is the narrative of the heart.

AUGUST

Monday August 6

The steroidal anti-inflammatory Decadron dose was reduced by 2mg on Thursday. You're now taking 32 mg: 8 mg more than physicians like to prescribe, but it's palliative care and if that's the dose you need to be yourself then that's the dose you need. When the psychiatrist dramatically reduced the dose before, you started falling. One of the nasty side effects with Decadron is that muscle atrophies, something they neglected to mention and a truth you literally stumbled upon. Your legs and calves are half the size they were in May. An obvious reminder of wasting away and the cancer's ravenous, insatiable progress.

Yet, today, you are much steadier on your feet, only reaching for the cane as insurance once you're weary. You've even been going for early morning dips in Iris's pool two yards over, Deb doing her 60 lengths of sanity and you floating about in the cool chemical blue on a pink noodle, a summer marvel of physics. When that is all there is, it is enough.

Alexander hand delivered the DVD of the roast the school alum held on your May birthday to raise the seed money for the Richard Holdsworth/Tarragon Theatre Fellowship. He is a divining rod of energy and you felt by being with him that you could recharge yourself, plug into the source and bring yourself back from the planet of exhaustion where you've been held prisoner for days.

I know you've since watched the DVD and that the satire pleased you and that the tender affection former students expressed surprised you in its candor and degree. You had believed you were just another teacher and you've discovered you meant much more to McPherson, Robertson, and Burnes and so many others you directed on stage and worked with on the sound and lighting design crews from *Bye Bye Birdie* to *The York Cycle* to *Never Look Back* to *Burlap Bags* to *A Midsummer Night's Dream* to *A Funny Thing Happened on the Way to the Forum*.

McPherson suggested that with *Never Look Back*—a detested musical by the boys in which your lead lost his voice on the second night and while you improvised his lines, Doug (as musical director) sang his songs—you *"lit a piece of shit on fire and everyone loved the smell."* Talk about the work of an alchemist! Enough to rival Ben Jonson's eponymous play. McPherson also recalled being in your class for the first time and assuming because of your flamboyance that you were gay; but *"when he told us about his wife and daughters, I thought, cool, Mr. Holdsworth is gay AND crafty."* That line had you roaring a personal laugh track, a trademark and infectious behavior known to anyone who sat in the same audience as you at any play at home in Toronto, at Shaw or Stratford or even on Broadway.

At the end of that evening on May 26 while we shared a birthday bottle of chilled Marlborough sauvignon blanc *chez vous,* the boys sang a suitably raucous version of *Happy Birthday* and raised their bottles cheering your name: a genuine, warm-hearted, adorable gesture.

Your friend Peter has managed to get your father's archival Super 8 family films onto DVD as well and you are looking forward to seeing those bears again that you and your sister Elizabeth fed cans of Coca Cola to in the late 1950s, up near Calendar where the Dionne quints were on display in the 1940s.

We ate lean burgers tonight sprinkled with Pusateri spices and grilled dutifully by Heather and Alice taking turns tending the new BBQ. There was a cool breeze under the shade of the cherry tree, made cooler by the bottle of pale pink Grenache and hunks of watermelon: a summer feast.

You showed me the peach oleander that has grown from the slip that you stole in Florence outside the church with the massive Caravaggio canvas depicting the martyrdom of St. Peter. You secreted it in a damp sock when it was only a few leaves on a stem. Now it is a sturdy little tree with gorgeous peach blossoms blushing open with red veins. Only six years later. This progress after you sang to it in its infancy, to no avail and finally got mad at it and planted it in a mixture of sand, peat and growth hormone and brought it inside through the winter months to be convinced by radiant heat.

We went for a walk around the Islington Golf Course that backs on to your property, a post-prandial stroll led by Deb stomping at the head of the line with determination to get you exercised. The cicadas in full-throated hum, wires buzzing, as the sun dipped to the horizon. You were steady on your pins even when a German shepherd-border collie-cross flew herding circles around us, kindly lit with a glow-in-the-dark flickering blue ball bobbing around its shaggy neck.

Alice came home early from Ontario Pioneer Camp where she has been a counselor assigned to a special needs camper who doesn't talk, feed herself, or toilet herself. Do anything, really. Though Alice was weary of being peed on, most of her clothes soiled, she wondered if the young girl perhaps demonstrated "*the purest form of living*." Besides, you are mentally in good shape these days and she doesn't want to miss an opportunity for real conversation with you where you are entirely engaged and responsive. Her countdown for University of Guelph has started. She's due in residence on Sunday September 2nd. Less than a month away. A moment from now and an eternity.

The Holdsworth clan will make the trek to Stratford this Thursday to see *Oklahoma!* at the Festival Theatre. It's brilliantly staged and choreographed by Donna Feore. You are going to beam throughout the evening as I did. It's amazing how that libretto has seeped into popular culture consciousness. I knew the words to most of the songs without even understanding how I knew them. I've goaded you into singing along with me,

> *There's a bright golden haze on the meadow.*
> *The corn is as high as a elephant's eye.*
> *And it looks like it's climbing right up to the sky.*
> *Oh what a beautiful mornin'*
> *Oh what a beautiful day*
> *I've got a wonderful feelin'*
> *Everything's goin' my way.*

How did two New York Jews—Richard Rodgers and Oscar Hammerstein—know so much about the cornfields of the Midwest? And what about . . .

> *Everything's up to date in Kansas City.*
> *They've gone about as far as you can go.*

Built a skyscraper seven stories high,
'bout as high as a building oughta grow.

or the sparring instructional imperative between Curly and Laurie as they lay claim to their nascent love for each other in the subtext:

Don't throw bouquets at me.
Don't praise my folks too much.
Don't laugh at my jokes too much.
People will say we're in love.

These Rodgers and Hammerstein lyrics and melodies are anthems to me and all the other musical theatre sluts. You included. The tunes and words will rush in like the fools they are when you're sitting in the Festival Theatre watching a real surrey with the fringe on the top move from stage right to stage left as Dan Chameroy's ebullient Curly woos Blythe Wilson's cautiously playful Laurie. And you will be charmed. Utterly charmed and transported to a gentler time.

Thursday August 9

We managed to go out for lunch this afternoon, at a delightful little bistro not far from your place on Islington. The soundtrack to get us there was the hilariously irreverent *Avenue Q*. Since you were unfamiliar with the show, other than knowing it was done with puppets who parodied characters on *Sesame Street*, I played you the titular song which begins with the following lyrics that could so easily have applied to our early professional lives:

What do you do with a B.A. in English?
What is my life going to be?
Four years of college and plenty of knowledge have earned me this
*   useless degree.*
. . . But somehow I can't shake the feeling I might make a difference to
*   the human race.*

And, you rewarded me with an exploding guffaw that had you coughing and weeping with delight. We sat in the car, air-conditioning blasting, until we played through another naughty piece called *"It Sucks to Be Me,"* a theme song you could embrace.

At the restaurant while I was placing our order, I ran into a former student who asked me what I was doing there. When I explained you and I were out for a bite to eat because you were having a good day, he became excited and craned his neck to try to see you. When I brought him over to our table, where you'd propped your cane on the back of my chair, his face fell for a nanosecond, acknowledging how much you have physically deteriorated from your formerly robust self. You immediately made him feel completely at ease by extending your hand in greeting and asking him about his summer plans and his face lit with recognition and understanding that you continue to care.

Familiar with your appreciation of bawdy lyrics, on the drive back to your house after a lunch of roast beef sandwiches on freshly baked, warm-from-the-oven olive focaccia, we listened to *The 25th Annual Putnam County Spelling Bee*, a show you'd considered producing at the school when the directing responsibility rotated once again to you. When the previous year's spelling champion is the first contestant to be eliminated, he sings the following earnest lament that had the audience at Circle in the Square in NYC where I saw it last summer choking in their seats with hysterics, tears streaming down their faces.

Teaching at a school for boys, as we have done, the piece has particular resonance. You'd even decided the boy you would cast in the role of Chip Tolantino who would unashamedly belt:

My unfortunate protuberance
seems to have its own exuberance
Anyone for M & M's? Delicious and appropriate.
Anyone for Chewy Goobers? Inexpensive.
Anyone for buying the shit that I'm selling?
Because my stiffy has ruined my spelling.

Not a day passes at the Royal School where any number of boys readjusts their testicles in full view in any location, completely oblivious, and mostly ignored by his classmates, unless, of course, he happens to be a serial offender. And then, as you know, they are unforgiving in their attention and suggest regardless of their audience, *"Johnson, keep both hands on your desk. What you're doing should be done in the privacy of your own home. Or at least alone. I don't want to see you whacking off. It isn't natural."* Oh, to have the unfiltered clarity of a teenage boy.

Thursday August 16

You had fretted about the sound portrait interview with Alannah, but she assures me that you both had a splendid time for hours this morning before she had to scurry away for you to be able to get to your scheduled session at Princess Margaret. You are a natural storyteller, a perfect subject, willing to be candid and unabashedly honest. All she had to do was prompt you with some of the anecdotes I prepped her with and you were off to the races, delighted to be yourself and to have a captive audience.

In addition to the music that you have selected to compliment the tone of the piece, Alannah is going to reformat a recording of you singing two hymns circa 1961 in your clear treble voice, a bonus disc that Alice and Heather will surely treasure.

Thursday August 30

With classes beginning next week after Labor Day, the rhythm of your Fall is no longer routine. Like me, you've spent the last weeks of many Augusts preparing for incoming students, a swell of hopefulness that we will be able to nurture in some of them a passion for the written word. Since you are officially on long-term disability because of the unpredictability of your glioblastoma, your end of summer planning has altered to include your current notion of enrolling in a watercolor class and finally learning how to capture the images of the flowers blooming in your garden, a skill surely different from slapping on broad strokes of oil paint for props and backdrops throughout years of school plays: the forest of Arden, pre-Christian Rome, early 20th century mid-western America, and the Garden of Eden.

SEPTEMBER

Sunday September 2

You and Deb packed Alice and her durable plastic bins exploding with clothes and books into your big green boat of a car to get her settled in her residence room at the University of Guelph where she's enrolled in a variety of first year Arts courses. And, you are button-popping proud.

Monday September 17

This afternoon I dropped off the completed Sound Portrait CDs that Alannah mixed of your interview and your treble solos. Your voice is now recorded nattering and chattering about your early years and about how much being a family with Deb and your daughters has meant to you since you never discovered who your birth parents were. Kiki, your familiar these days, your "*ivory and blue tail-feathered bitch,*" was out of her cage, perched often on the curtain rods down which she was gleefully shitting pellets that rolled off the heavy golden shot silk. She was none too pleased with me and exercised her disdain by dive-bombing me in the chair. A tiny pterodactyl.

You've hurt your back somehow by stretching absolutely the wrong way. And, it is that inflammation that has you stuck in bed. Not the cancer. I forced an ice pack wrapped in a dish-towel on you and it gave a little immediate relief. We shared mugs of orange blossom herbal tea and I read you the opening of Elizabeth Hay's *Late Nights on Air*, a contender for this year's Scotiabank Giller Prize.

I know you thoroughly delighted in her previous novel *Garbo Laughs*, because of the protagonist's obsession with old films, especially those with a fresh-faced Frank Sinatra. The opening paragraph of the new one is enough to transcend this time and place and feel cozied up by the fire in Hay's narrative. As I read to you which you are keen for me to do, I also drift to that evocative northern landscape:

Harry was in his little house on the edge of Back Bay when at half past twelve her voice came over the radio for the first time. A voice unusual in its sound and unusual in itself, since there were no other female announcers on air. He listened to the slow, clear, almost unnatural confidence, the low-pitched sexiness, the elusive accent as she read the local news. More than curious, already in love, he walked into the station the next day at precisely the same time.

OCTOBER

Wednesday October 10

We've just put Thanksgiving weekend to rest and Deb and the girls got you up and out of your bed to join the Petersons and their extended clan for the traditional turkey and all of the trimmings. You raved about Iris's cooking and worried about how hosting such a meal exhausts her now that she's in her eighties, even though she absolutely insists on doing it with little-to-no help from her own children. Iris and Len have been surrogate parents to you and grandparents to Alice and Heather, the only grandparents they've known. They are both wrecked with the idea of your certain death.

You are too exhausted to even entertain the idea of a conversation, so I read to you from *Me and Orson Welles*, a charming little novel written by Robert Kaplow that is set in NYC in the 1930s when the garrulous and talented twenty-something actor/director was mounting his anti-fascist production of *Julius Caesar* at the Mercury Theatre. The protagonist is a seventeen-year-old Brooklynite named Richard who dreams of the acting life and by happenstance finds himself strumming a lute and acting as a sidekick to Welles as they get the production ready for opening night. As I tried out different voices and attitudes, blustery for Welles, Jewish New Yorker à la Mel Brooks for Richard, poncy Brit for John Houseman—who WAS a poncy Brit—you guffawed and chortled and eased yourself into rest, eyes shut, smiling broadly, with your occasional critical commentary, smatterings of *"that's WON-der-ful," "how MAR-vel-lous"* and *"he's SO clever,"* stretching out your vowels for emphasis and delight in the sound of your own voice.

When you finished dozing we talked about the ramps you intend to have built throughout the house to facilitate mobility in the wheelchair or with the walker on wheels, like a sophisticated set you were accustomed to designing as a director of so many plays. *The York Cycle* was your most impressive attempt and most foolish and most successful of those in my time with you at RSGC. You convinced our headmaster to remove the pews and to construct scaffolding in the chapel to turn it into an arena for the production that involved almost every boy in the school. Only you could pull off that organizational nightmare.

I happily directed "Noah and the Flood," one of fifteen short plays presented, and used the theme song from *Mister Rogers' Neighborhood* to get the Junior School boys onto the stage:

> *It's a beautiful day in the neighborhood, a beauteous day for a*
> *   neighbor*
> *Would you be mine? Could you be mine?*
> *. . . Won't you, please? Won't you, please?*
> *Please, won't you be my neighbor.*

Then "Splish Splash" became the piece on which to hang one of their dance sequences once it starts to pour after the animals are safely aboard the ark and the dove is sent out to find the olive branch—the proof of solid ground and the chance for a new beginning.

Your brain is starting to trick you, though you are blissfully unaware. When I commented on how late in the season it was to see golf carts puttering by at the foot of your lawn, you assured me, "*Heavens, no, we're just gearing up for summer here in New Zealand.*" So, I play along, abandoning the impulse to correct you, ignoring my need to be right.

Tuesday October 16

I am buzzing with excitement for tomorrow night's PEN Canada fundraiser with Scottish crime writer Ian Rankin appearing in conversations with Margaret Atwood that I've co-chaired with Ellen S. You've just finished reading one of her authors' books: Michael Ondaatje's *Divisadero*, a dark and brooding novel. I wonder how many more books you'll be able to savor on your own from the growing pile at your bedside: *Mister Pip, Still Life, The Assassin's Song, All That Matters.*

I've promised to remember all the hot bits of the opening night of the International Festival of Authors and report back next week. I'm meeting Ian Rankin tonight at an event that his publisher is hosting at Dora Keogh—the Canadian launch of his final Rebus novel, *Exit Music*. And, the title, of course, makes me think of your exit music. Wondering what you have planned because I know you and Giles and Doug met in the late summer when you were in good form. Then you were yet entirely yourself, though easily tired after a walk to the end of the garden, your gnarled walking stick gripped in your right hand, your uncompromised side.

Now, during my visits with you, although I'd love to get you outside since it is unseasonably warm, even though you insist to Deb that I have taken you each time I come by the house, the furthest I've managed is to get you with your walker on its sturdy rubber wheels to the main floor toilet. It's a short thirty-foot journey, but one that exhausts you, nonetheless. So tires you that you have me haul up your sweatpants once you're off the porcelain god, because that is an effort that is beyond your capacity, though you have managed to wipe your own ass this time, a small mercy, drenched in sweat and focused as you are at getting safely back to your living room bed.

Dignity is something this stage of your cancer no longer affords you or your girls. There is no bathroom door on the ground floor because there is simply not enough room to maneuver to the toilet with one since you rely on the cumbersome walker for stability and what's left of your independence. Was it only in March that you took Alice and Heather cross-country skiing and enjoyed the bracing air in the eastern townships of Quebec and the physicality of cutting fresh trails through the hardened crust of snow?

Kiki-the-budgie continues to be too smart for me, for just as I think to slam the little wire door to her cage, she chirps and swoops out to perch on the curtain rod above you and wait for you to try to engage her in avian discourse of cheeps and trills, which you do. Threatening her all the while with the idea of an interloper, you chide her about her behavior and suggest you'll replace her with "*a great macaque, dressed in black blue plumage with a ruby chest and the ability to chat about Beckett or Pinter.*" Another familiar to *while away the hours conferring with the flowers, consulting with the rain . . .* You'd unravel every riddle for any individual in trouble or in pain.

Wednesday October 22

Your dear friend Peter was sitting on the sofa when I arrived mid-day with the food provided by one of the many school families who have been feeding your family since your diagnosis. Catherine M. has managed to organize a variety of nutritious offerings including pasta Bolognese, marinated pork tenderloin, maple-soaked salmon, Irish stew and spanakopita in portions that even appeal to adolescent girls who pick at their servings like little birds.

I was able to flit about, clean up the kitchen under your booming direction from the next room, brew a pot of herbal tea, and then find a bottle of red wine to uncork while Peter left to try and get takeout banquet burgers from a local pub. In September the two of you strolled there, but that is impossible now, a notion entrenched in your past. Waiting for Peter's return we had a little sip of a robust Australian cabernet sauvignon, a delicious indulgence so early on a weekday. What is time anyway.

Peter came back the conquering hero and the two of you feasted on the meal, you with the meat juice dripping from your chin, happily dipping your home-cut French fries in ketchup and mayonnaise, no longer worried about extra calories or ever watching your waistline again, as you sat perched at the edge of your bed, Peter, delicately holding his tie to his chest with his left hand, napkins at the ready, to pat the corners of his mouth.

You were in excellent form, though feeling rather debilitated and distracted by your ongoing back pain. Dr. P., your palliative care doctor, has been by to readjust the pain meds, but you told me *"I haven't been completely honest with him regarding the intensity of my pain because I worry that stronger dosages will make me dopey. I'm used to looking like Dopey, but I'm holding on to my wit for as long as I can."* I understand that reticence to give in to the treatment if it might compromise your intellect. Your refusal to be honest about your pain is making Deb crazy, because it is up to her to try to settle you at three in the morning when you are moaning in genuine agony. She hates that you are pretending to be brave and assures you that it's certainly not necessary for her sake. Denying pain doesn't make you more of a man.

As promised, I gave you my play-by-play version of Ian Rankin's visit to Toronto, beginning with the McArthur & Company *fête* at Dora Keogh on the Danforth, where our progressive mayor, David Miller, thrilled to talk cities with one of Edinburgh's most famous residents. When I was introduced to Rankin, I was surprised by the soft plushness of his handshake, verging on timid, though admittedly he had a firm grip on his pint of Guinness. I couldn't blame him in such a crowded room where, famous or not, it might take awhile to secure the next glass of stout.

Rankin admitted that he has a home on "Writer's Block" in Edinburgh near fellow Scottish novelists Alexander McCall Smith and J.K. Rowling of the stratospheric *Harry Potter* fame. My friend Alison G., another crime writer, who has known him for over twenty years, confirms that he is as sweet as he seems. As if to prove her point, in her copy of the final Rebus novel he scrawled "*For Alison, all my unrequited love.*"

The following evening Ian Rankin appeared in conversation with Margaret Atwood at Premiere Dance Theatre at the opening night of the International Festival of Authors/PEN Canada fundraiser that I co-chaired. In addition to being casually handsome and entirely at ease in his own skin as he slouched in his chair, Rankin was engaging on stage as he bantered with the erudite and witty Booker-Prize-winning Atwood who had prepared questions for him based on *Exit Music*. Atwood was adept at getting Rankin to talk about his appointment by the Lord Provost of Edinburgh to be an official host, should H.M. Queen Elizabeth II visit. When prodded about where he would take Her Majesty, Rankin quickly responded, "*to the Oxford Bar, of course, but since the Queen is notoriously skint without cash on hand, I'd be left to buy the rounds.*"

You'll be amused to know that he is working on the libretto for a 15-minute opera competition in 2008 and hopes to place a respectable second, to be relieved of the obligation to produce the full score should he and his composer partner regrettably be named the winners.

Thursday October 30

I didn't expect to see Alice sitting on the living room sofa, legs tucked up underneath her, nursing a bowl of soup this afternoon, since she has been having such a fabulous start to her first year at Guelph. I took her to the local walk-in clinic off Dundas West to pick up her blood test results that were being faxed from the university health centre and now she's being treated for mono. The MD has given her a note excusing her from two weeks of classes/assignments with the expectation that she will seem tired and sluggish for the next month. She seems to be taking the news in stride, unsurprised, really, so that means Deb will have both you and Alice at home in bed convalescing. It's a good thing Deb admittedly has a "*hearty constitution,*" such an old-fashioned thing to say.

I delivered a care package of your favorite things from colleagues: a selection of exquisite cheese, dry sherry, smokey single malt scotch with a hint of peat, watercolor brushes and a Fellini DVD. Tim H. found a rare copy of the 1974 Academy Award-winning *Amarcord*, which thrilled you then and thrills you now in its carnivalesque portrait of provincial Italy during the Fascist period. The enduring cinema classic is Fellini's most personal film satirizing his youth and turning daily life into a circus of social rituals, adolescent desires, male fantasies and political subterfuge. It is decidedly up your alley, pandering to your intellect and your contrived cultural snobbishness.

NOVEMBER

Wednesday November 7

I've finally caught up with Deb after an extended game of telephone tag and she tells me that the past few days have been a real rollercoaster emotionally because you were in distress and having difficulty breathing on Sunday night and she called an ambulance to get you to the hospital. Turns out the pulmonary embolism that you experienced in the summer has re-emerged and you needed IV meds to adjust the blood thinner level to help break the clot down in an effort to avoid another vacuuming. You're at Trillium in Mississauga again until further notice.

Deb has been grateful to have both of your girls together at home, though Alice is feeling better and planning to return to school on the weekend. They sat on the kitchen floor one night this week, stuffing themselves sick with Hallowe'en candy, sucking on gooey candy kisses, talking and weeping.

Sunday November 11

Heather's been reading to you from *Peter Pan*, a beautiful little payback for all the sleepless evenings you read that very book to her when she was a little girl determined to stay up through the night. I told Deb I would come and spend some time with you today so she could go to the Tarragon Theatre with your friend Donna this afternoon to see the new play *East of Berlin*. On my drive along the Gardiner and the Queen Elizabeth Way I was listening to Michael Enright's Sunday morning program on CBC Radio One and he played the recording of Scottish actor John Hanna reading W.H. Auden's *"Funeral Blues"* from *Four Weddings and a Funeral*. And, as I find myself considering the days left to you on this earth, and the days ahead for your girls, it occurs to me that this beautiful and provocative poem would begin to articulate Deb's imagined loss of you.

Funeral Blues

Stop all the clocks, cut off the telephone.
Prevent the dog from barking with a juicy bone,
Silence the pianos and with muffled drum
Bring out the coffin, let the mourners come.

. . . The stars are not wanted now; put out every one,
Pack up the moon and dismantle the sun.
Pour away the ocean and sweep up the wood;
For nothing now can ever come to any good.

Auden understood endings and how they could gut the living left behind.

Deb and Alice and Heather were in Room 413 when I got there around 11:30 this morning, you holding court as best as you can, being sure to introduce each person who passes behind your curtain. You are Oz with a little bit of magic left yet. And, ever considerate. I am astonished to bear witness to the good manners at your core. You thank every nurse who comes by your bed for being so attentive. Even when they're not.

On some level you know that you are dying, yet you behave as though it were your remotest concern. To paraphrase Morrie Schwartz in *Tuesdays with Morrie*, you're not as alive as you used to be, but you're not yet dead.

You're somewhere in between.

I am learning from you that we always have a choice and I am reminded of the final verse in *Always Look on the Bright Side of Life* from *Spamalot*:

Life is quite absurd, and death's the final word.
You must always face the curtain with a bow!
Forget about your sin. Give the audience a grin.
Enjoy it, it's your last chance anyhow!

Two weeks ago you confessed that you felt your death approaching. Circling round. Snuffling its way to you, unthreatening like your childhood dog Spice, a chocolate lab-cross who spent years snuggled beside you through the lonely nights in small-town Ontario. "*Like a hedgehog, a benign cuddly creature,*" you said. And you are unafraid. When one of the many pastoral care workers asked if you felt comfortable with your belief in God and an afterlife, you claimed, "*Sure. Sure. We're fine.*"

This morning you were preoccupied with the notion of getting to Kilimanjaro to make the treacherous ascent on foot, but I tried to dissuade you from that pursuit by suggesting that there was a current shortage of sherpas to guide us up the mount. That seemed to suffice as a reasonable response, and you were off on another discourse about Mayan turquoise this time, triggered by the color of the plastic line attached to the light above your bed for you to tug to summon nursing attention.

Another hospital chaplain dropped by your bed and asked if she could offer a prayer for you. You quickly responded, "*Of course. Sure. Sure.*" No sooner had she launched into a rote contemplation, her tiny prayer book held in one palm, you began toying with the buttons on your bed, adjusting your position and then the prayer itself as you began mimicking the rhythm of her words with your schoolboy Latin opening of the Lord's Prayer: *Pater Noster, qui est in caelis.* Your recitation soon morphed into fake Latin, though delivered with the equal earnestness as you caught my eye, winked, and continued wickedly, "*flatulence, botulism, benedictus.*" Trying not to fall to the floor in hysterics, I interrupted your performance imploring in a line stolen from Elizabeth I in Timothy Findley's *Elizabeth Rex*: "*will no one say amen?*" You winked again and the chaplain chirped, "*Oh, yes, I will. Amen,*" releasing us from the absurdity of the moment you conjured.

I've been reading to you anecdotes from David Sedaris's collection *Me Talk Pretty One Day* and managed to coax a vintage chortle out of you from the piece about taking French classes in Paris where Sedaris is baffled by the masculine and feminine assignations to nouns that seem so arbitrary: "*What's the trick to remembering a sandwich is masculine? What quality does it share with anyone in possession of a penis?*" A fair enough question, we agree.

Monday November 12

Doug just rang to tell me about his visit with you this afternoon and how distressed he felt on your behalf. He tried to get you out of the room in the wheelchair for a change of scenery and to have a peek at the paintings hung on the second floor done by Susie, a young woman who used to baby sit Heather and Alice. You could last about 15 minutes and then the pain in your back, from the disintegrating bone, chewed to chalky bits by the steroids, was just too much and he got you back to your bed and convinced one of the nurses to give you a shot of painkiller to give you some relief.

This "incident" pain has your medical team baffled, but nevertheless it makes me cross that you aren't medicated without having to request it to at least take the edge off. You've got to keep ahead of the waves of pain, because once they hit, it takes too long for any relief. There is no reason for you to continue suffering in this way.

Once the medicine relaxed you in warm waves, you just about made Doug wet himself with a comment about the school administration when you suggested, "*if I were to cast Richard III using faculty there, James could play the hump.*" Ever the wit. And I mean EVER. That playfulness and your good manners are at the core of who you are.

Doug said you were entertaining him with great swaths of Dickens in imaginary reconstructed conversations between Pip and Magwitch in *Great Expectations*, better suited for the script of the *South Park* parody where Estella harvests the tears of the young men whose hearts she has broken to fuel her "Genesis device." Surprisingly, Dickens hasn't made the cut of one of the books stacked in your hospital room.

For company you have *T.S. Eliot The Collected Poems*: no other poet could make you feel so immediately better about your own lot in life than the moribund TSE rattling on about *"hurry up please, it's time;" Good News for Modern Man*, that yellow and black dust-jacketed, watered-down version of the New Testament popular with confirmation classes because of the cartoon illustrations; and *Mister Pip* (the spark for the Dickensian rumination, I suspect) by New Zealand native Lloyd Jones, short listed for this year's Booker Prize and snubbed by Ireland's Anne Enright's winner, *The Gathering*, which I am currently reading at home.

In its opening chapter, Veronica, the narrator, confesses, *"I wait for the kind of sense that dawn makes, when you have not slept. I stay downstairs while the family breathes above me and I write it down, I lay them out in nice sentences, all my clean, white bones."* In recent weeks you have waited for that same kind of sense to bloom in your chest.

You'd find Enright's novel worthy of your AP Literature course. A companion piece for Virginia Woolf's *Mrs. Dalloway* or Michael Cunningham's *The Hours*. A distinctly female perspective that you understood was critical to offer up to the boys as they continue to navigate their messy way through relationships with the women in their lives: mothers, sisters, daughters, lovers, and friends.

You've also made plenty of room for playfulness in those classes, especially Senior Drama where Florez has entered, hands poised to clap as if he were the most practiced Flamenco dancer, claiming, *"don't doubt it boys. I am my own party. Besides, being a narcoleptic would be too exhausting."* And where Martin marveled at a prop box find: *"Have you seen this fur coat? Give me a pair of pink star-framed glasses and I'll be set."* Florez responded, *"Awesome, possum. You know, I heard Diablo*

Cody wrote the screenplay for Juno *with a pen squeezed between her butt cheeks."*

There's nothing like a boys' school for embracing drag. Almost any one of them will throw out their arms with glee at the opportunity to borrow a girlfriend's kilt or tunic and slap on a tube of Revlon Red lipstick in order to pout for the yearbook camera and posterity.

Thursday November 15

When I got to Trillium today, Deb told me that you were groggy from sedation and you chimed in, *"what station? Am I at Grand Central Station? No wonder I'm confused. At Grand Central Station, I often sit down and weep."* You and Elizabeth Smart.

Your medical team had intended to do a colonoscopy this morning (having tortured you with the prep last night and put you in a diaper), but then abandoned the notion for no particular reason. Jesus, Mary and Joseph! That certain unnecessary cruelty makes my Irish temper flare and I fantasize about slugging someone in the hospital who thought such an invasive procedure a good idea at this stage.

How can that possibly contribute to your comfort? Word is that it's only clear fluids by mouth today with another attempt planned tomorrow morning. I wish I'd thought to bring a sup of single malt Scotch, instead of the iced cappuccino that you are slurping so enthusiastically. This is a problem, I see, of not being in a palliative care unit where the medical staff will coddle you and make your final days as calming as possible.

The official word from Princess Margaret Hospital, where you have asked to go when you are ready to die, is that they take clients with two weeks or less left; there is such demand for their palliative care unit where spirits soar. How will you know? How will Deb know? How will your doctors know? It is guesswork at best.

You're back on an IV—a saline drip, though you're not worrying the port today like you were on my weekend watch. You managed to yank it out and bloody your bedclothes in an aborted attempt to scratch an unscratchable itch on your vellum skin. The mechanical bed has your attention again and you make me dizzy as you adjust and readjust, head up, feet down, feet up, head down. The cicada buzz of the hydraulics with each button push. A Royal wave as you sit back up and get the angle just right.

Your current roommate, a crotchety 80-year-old war vet who has left his hearing aid at his daughter's place, and as stubborn as he is unsteady on his feet, confounds you.

You can't seem to process that you are not at home. Even when you are assured, *"Richard, you are in the hospital and the voices you hear are the nurses and orderlies in the hallway outside your room,"* you just won't accept it as the truth. And, when the conversation through the track curtain becomes annoying you furrow your brow and stage whisper to me, *"Who ARE these people? Can't I simply have a quiet afternoon left alone to read in bliss? To listen to the radio without all of these interruptions?"*

Today I brought Stuart McLean's *Stories from the Vinyl Café* to dip into and to help you pass the afternoon. He plans to put together a package for you of his CDs where he reads stories from several collections along with a note where he explains how much joy he had from the theatrical productions you mounted over the years he was part of the RSGC community. You even directed his son as love-struck Lysander in *A Midsummer Night's Dream*, a role in which art imitated his father's life.

Before I began the hilarious *"Polly Anderson's Christmas Party"* where Morley is shamed by Polly's sushi crèche with the wasabi-faced wisemen, you reminisced about being read to as a child. Believing that *Winnie the Pooh* was the first book you remember being read from by your mother. Though, it could have been *Peter Pan*. You certainly read both books to Alice and Heather when they were little girls. The rhythm and cadence of stories soothe you. Even now you imagine being tucked under a quilt, a fire crackling in the hearth. Smiling, you lose yourself in the lilt of the narrative.

A physiotherapist came in to do an assessment and you chatted invitingly to her. *"Yes, of course, one of my immediate goals is to get out of this bed and strengthen my legs for long walks with my wife through the changing colors up by the McMichael Gallery. We do it every Fall. Walk through those glorious Group of Seven landscapes and try to match the canvases hanging on the walls."*

I'm beginning to wonder if any of these support care workers are reading your chart. You are still convincing in conversation because of your immense vocabulary and theatrical delivery and I believe that this particular young woman actually thought she'd get you sitting up on the edge of your bed and moving out the door with a walker this afternoon, when the sad truth is you haven't been out of bed in weeks except to be transferred to a commode or a wheelchair. You had your last bath in a real tub a week ago.

You admitted to her that though you have been preoccupied with doing that very thing that you were ashamed to admit that you no longer felt compelled. You don't feel it is possible with your current pain to get out of bed at all. They've been checking your vitals regularly this afternoon, because of wonky blood pressure. First at 15-minute intervals, then at thirty, and now every hour. The next at 15:10. Hospitals run on military time.

I've asked your advice about visiting Paris where I hope to travel in March and you tell me that I must spend loads of time strolling along the Seine. Not rushing anywhere. Dipping into cafés in the morning along the *quai* for a large bowl of steaming *café au lait* and a flakey croissant. Or settling down with a *pichet de vin rouge* and a crusty baguette filled with brie in the *après midi*. You help me dream an itinerary that includes: *Le Select* and *Les Deux Magots,* bistros where Canadian novelist Morley Callaghan loitered to meet his boxing rival Ernest Hemingway and *The Great Gatsby* novelist Scott Fitzgerald in the 1920s; *Shakespeare & Co.*, the old-fashioned bookshop with floor-to-ceiling shelves stuffed with English-language titles, originally owned by Sylvia Beach who daringly published Joyce's *Ulysses*; *Montmartre's Père La Chaise* cemetery where it's *de rigeur* to smooch, lips ruby red, Jacob Epstein's fine stone monument designed to mark Oscar Wilde's place and where Ireland's ex-pat playwright is in good company with Jim Morrison, the legendary front man of *The Doors*, writer Gertrude Stein and dancer Isadora Duncan. You quip, "*poor Isadora, she's not dancing nearly as well as she used to.*" Well, no she's not, having died in 1927. Your last word on Paris is that it is essential to adopt an intrinsically French sensibility, *mais bien sûr.*

Jennifer from the Dorothy Lay hospice dropped by, and you were pleased to see her and began to plan a lovely afternoon of wine tasting in the perennial garden at Sunset House. Lobster canapés and other *amuse bouche*, crisp chilled white wine, greens from the vegetable beds for a freshly picked salad. A lovely comforting vision that mirrors actual evenings I've spent in your backyard with other friends at the long table dressed in a lemon and indigo Provençale print, under the fragrant cherry tree. Hold on to that thought.

Tuesday November 20

John K. stopped in for a visit on his way back to Meaford and you were self-deprecating as you suggested to him that, with your swollen face and virtually hairless head, you most resemble Dopey from *Snow White and the Seven Dwarfs*. When I asked you how you found John, you replied, as if you were talking about yourself, "*I was surprised he was so coherent. Even talking in tenses of the future.*"

Wednesday November 21

You had a psychotic episode on Monday. You were genuinely terrified and believed your food had been laced with narcotics: visions of Russell Crowe's dramatic breakdown in *A Beautiful Mind*. You insisted through a series of screams that a siege was underway, and you were the intended target: Troy before the sack. When you emerged from the horror of writhing from side-to-side incapable of accepting reality, Deb assured you that she believed you were a pretty good couple through your years together and you upped the ante and asserted, "*I think we're stunning.*"

Today you are considerably less anxious and not overtly paranoid, your engaging self. Your dreamscape is rich and varied and apparently inhabited by people you've known. Like me.

You've dreamed me into the life of a Himalayan cat who owns a bookshop in Old Montreal, that stocks only the most auspicious French titles including Guy de Maupassant's "The Necklace," Françoise Sagan's jewel *Bonjour Tristesse,* and Baudelaire's *Fleurs du Mal.* You remind me that, *malheureusement*, the joke's on me because I don't speak a whit of French. I implore that at the very least you will take pity and teach me to swear convincingly with a litany of an occasional *tabernacle* or *sacre bleu*! But you dismiss my request and move unexpectedly into contemplating T.S. Eliot's *The Cocktail Party* and that old widow, *Veuve Cliquot,* which navigates us predictably to a Cole Porter ditty in *High Society*:

> *Have you heard; it's almost dawn?*
> *Mow the bubbly and pour the lawn*
> *Well, did you evah?*
> *What a swell party this is*

Your hospital bed is proving a mechanical challenge today as you try to figure out the best position in which to rest your fractured back. Pressing the buttons, arrow up, arrow down. Head higher. Feet lower. Complaining all the while about *"the howler monkeys who vocalize mostly jaw and windpipe and screech through my skull."* The cancer in your brain isn't the source of your pain that has you rolling from side to side, but the deteriorated vertebrae that have been chewed to chalky fragments by the steroids prescribed to reduce the swelling of the tumors.

The most frustrating scenario to witness is the nursing staff's insistence that you request your pain medication as needed. By the time you think to ask, it's too late to get ahead of your pain. Most days you don't even know if you've asked or taken any. Just now, I called back Nurse Kim and prompted you to ask for the narcotic and you're naughtily singing, *"A spoonful of Percocet helps the hallucinations go on, the hallucinations go o-on, the hallucinations go on."* Maybe that is why Mary Poppins was so chipper. Or found conversation with the parrot end of her umbrella so engaging.

Two nursing students from George Brown College stand at

the foot of your bed and in their lilting Caribbean accents ask you about hand washing protocol and you are happy to oblige them, and they nod approvingly until you confound them with your insistence that they mustn't confuse hand washing with an anti-bacterial alcoholic gel with scrubbing with Nutella. Have they heard? The word is out. You prefer to use *"Bombay gin from the bathtub spout,"* and finish the thought by mime-licking the residue between your splayed fingers. For your performance you are rewarded with tiny bottles of hand gel to share with your visitors, pledging all the while to demonstrate your unflappable technique.

You've got heartburn this afternoon and manage to depress the call button on your bedrail for Nurse Kim. She peers behind the curtain in minutes and says she'll get an order for milk of magnesia. When she returns, she warns that the creamy opaque liquid will not only settle the burning in your chest, but also help with a bowel movement and you assure her, *"I don't mind the idea of a good BM. It could be the highlight of my day. Don't abandon all hope, ye who enter here."*

Friday November 23

You've had a bad reaction to Haldon: an anticipated side effect of extreme restlessness that can lead to suicidal thoughts which you confide you've been having: *"entre nous, of course, Janet, you must understand, I've been thinking about putting an end to it all by jumping from the Bloor Street Viaduct. What a splendid splat I'd make. Ruining rush hour along the Don Valley. Time stops for no man, except for me on that day."* You are beside yourself with anxiety. Writhing in agony, it's like you're tap dancing on broken feet.

Saturday November 24

I'm taking the morning hospital visit shift so Deb can try to sleep in a little since Heather went to Guelph last night to stay with Alice and her university friends. Plus, yesterday just about did her in, having to see you in such distress. It is clear that all of the decisions forward now are hers and that responsibility numbs her.

When I arrived this morning as visiting hours began for non-family members at 9 a.m., you were sitting up, bare-chested, picking at your breakfast tray spread with varying degrees of mush. The turquoise plastic urine bottle, not quite full, upright to the left.

I'd brought an Americano from Starbucks and when I offered it to you, you beamed, "*ecco, si, multo bene, vino rosso, mille grazie.*" How can you retrieve Italian phrases, but not know that you are in a hospital? You are convinced that you are staying in a badly run noisy boutique hotel, and you're bang on about the badly run part. Already I've asked one of the nurses I haven't met to make sure that she is able to give you a sponge bath and clean you up before your wife arrives this afternoon. She will try, but she is "*awfully busy.*"

All drinks have to reach your mouth by bendy straws now and even then you manage to end up splashing yourself and the bedclothes. As far as I can tell, the mess does not bother you. It doesn't even register now, a stark contrast to your previous fastidiousness and predisposition for natty and expensive attire. You sit up, eyes bright, delighted to launch into any discourse. I'm the one with the problem of seeing you covered in remnants of your last two meals. Silently seething about your right to dignity.

Nurse Kim is on again and she is concerned about your breathing. She has listened to your gurgling lungs through her stethoscope and has brought you an injection to help with the congestion. Eva from housekeeping has come to pick up your tray and to tidy around your bed and her name has you on a tangent about *"the pickled Gabor sisters and their extensive collections of bad wigs and worse husbands."*

I ask about your favorite musicals and you are quick to reply that the best shows are *Guys and Dolls* and *Oklahoma* because *"the song lyrics drive the narrative and character development."* We can't resist bursting into *"Fugue for Tinhorns,"* one of Frank Loesser's songs given to Nicely-Nicely Johnson (the Stubby Kaye character in the Sinatra film version) while your new roommate, a 30-something man missing both legs, moans before his next morphine hit:

I'm picking Valentine 'cause on the morning line
A guy has got him figured at five to nine
Has chance, has chance,

This guy says the horse has chance
If he says the horse has chance,
has chance, has chance

I wish you had chance on your side.

Heather has left you a note propped on the frame of family photo collage, some snapped at her confirmation in May, others of you and Deb and Alice and Heather before you knew you were sick, all beaming broadly at the camera. You've always enjoyed mugging for the camera. The note is folded into itself, an exquisite origami envelope, and scribbled with lime green marker. You ask me to read it to you and I do and marvel at its sweetness and naïveté as Heather assures you in her teenish way, "*I had fun visiting you on Thursday night, Dad, and will see you again tonight when I return with Alice from Guelph. I love you.*" I try to refold it, but Heather will need to adjust it to fit perfectly again, a *billet-doux* from your littlest girl, a lovely blonde with a new bob (since she donated her much longer locks to a program that makes wigs for children with cancer), the legs of a racehorse and your cerulean eyes.

You call me closer to your bedside and confide that what you are about to disclose is strictly *entre nous*. You insist that you have been "*cryptically but intentionally disappearing in recent weeks because of my living nightmares. It is unlikely that I will hurt myself, though the thought has crossed my mind.*" You had hatched a plan.

Confiding to your wife that you are scared has helped. You harbor the delusion that you are seeing the head of psychiatry at PMH daily and that you need to, when the truth is you haven't left this bed at Trillium since you arrived almost three weeks ago on November 5th. You've also tried to assure Alice and Heather that their presence is part of your healing. Deb continues to be unwavering in her support: "*so strong for me,*" you insist.

"*Will you assure me that you will stand by her and support her through my death?*" This moment of clarity is right on the money. I promise.

In the next breath you are conjuring "Mister Creosote" in Monty Python's *The Meaning of Life* and demanding first the wafer-thin mint and then the bucket for the projectile vomiting to end all projectile vomiting spewing out of a high-pressure hose in the film. As you repeatedly move your coffee mug to the edge of your tray and then the Styrofoam cup of crushed ice and water, trying to fiddle each in its right place, you reminisce about the famous cook, Madame Benoit, "*this lovely Gaya, earth woman who is* la reine *of French cuisine*." You are adamant that she prepares a delectable turkey with Canada Dry ginger ale cans upended around the bird in a large pan, their fizzy sweetness infusing the meat and complimenting the roasting chunks of fresh ginger root. With no apparent segue you insist, "*If I'm going to play the role of martini mixer, I'm going to have to mix a little earlier.*" I request a vodka martini, shaken, not stirred, with a curl of lemon zest, and you swivel your head to locate the necessary ingredients before having a little unintended kip.

About an hour after Nurse Kim gave you the subcutaneous injection in your stomach, the site astonishingly recommended by most patients (when I associate it with painful treatment for rabies), you begin to doze in earnest and then slip into a deeper REM sleep. Your eyebrows raise and lower and your mouth twitches as I imagine you give in to your dreamscape, eyes tightly closed.

You have relaxed into the rhythm of a waltz, a steady 1-2-3 between breaths. There's a call bell that ding dongs, one-two, and the linen trolleys clatter in the hallway while the nurses chatter collegially, a counterpoint to the palpable dreariness on this ward.

I bend my head back to Barry Callaghan's exquisite short story collection *Between Trains* and read aloud from "Dog Days of Love" and even your agitated neighbor behind the flimsy hospital curtain settles as the touching tale of Father Wilson and his golden retriever Anselm unfurls.

I hear my name, swivel my neck and flutter my fingers at Deb in the doorway and mime that you are sleeping and join her out in the hall to find a spot to chat without the worry of waking you when you have been so restless.

Two months ago, you told me as you crept closer and closer to your death that you would sleep more: the wheel of life come full circle back to the demands of your infancy.

Deb is exhausted and frustrated by the pressure of decision-making that is now hers alone. Admittedly, she's lousy about deciding anything. You took that worry on when you married. Because of the fractures in your spine, there is an orthopedic surgeon who has been consulted who wants to puncture you and pump you full of cement, which he maintains is a pain-relieving measure, if it works. If it doesn't work, you won't feel any worse. So they say. You'll be face down on an operating table and have a local anesthetic to make the procedure endurable. It is a risk you agree to take if its projected success means you might get home to Sunset House for a few days.

Deb cries as we sit on the stiff and cracking burnt orange vinyl chairs outside the elevator. She is furious that you are not getting the death that the doctors promised both of you at the time of your diagnosis. That you would sleep more and more and gently slip away, sliding out of your atrophied body, as people with glioblastoma have been known to do. She feels betrayed by the medical establishment. She hung all her hopes and your hopes too on a comfortable, pain-free death. There remain two certainties, neither of them comforting: your unassuageable pain and your imminent death.

ACT THREE

Exit

Life kills. That is its purpose.

—Timothy Findley, *Elizabeth Rex*

Monday November 26

Deb has called to ask me to drive Alice to Guelph to retrieve her course books and clothes from her residence room. She believes your end is near. Earlier today you looked in her eyes as she leaned over your hospital bed, stroking your hand, and said *"Drippy drop"* as tears trailed down her face off the tip of her nose, staining your bedclothes. And, later, with Deb and Alice and Heather surrounding your bed, you closed your eyes and blurted, after hours of unresponsiveness, *"I'm traveling."* Alice joked, *"Where Dad? To the bank? To cash in on your incredible life?"* It may well be.

Tuesday November 27

Knowing I was driving Alice to pick up her stuff, I arranged for coverage of my classes where the Grade Elevens are knee deep in Louise Penny's *Dead Cold*—the most successful novel I've taught to 16-year-old boys—and my Writer's Craft students are typing away on their original short fiction pieces, some of which are influenced by Ian Rankin's perfectly constructed "The

Hanged Man." Earlier this morning Johnson popped in and perched cross-legged on a desk as he knitted a fuchsia pompom for one of his tea-cozy ski hats that are remarkably in high demand because he is an accomplished racer, a campy Madame Defarge wondering aloud, *"How much do you miss me, Ma'am? Bet there's a void in your life."* Before Writer's Craft, Fawkes talked through the topic of his personal essay for his applications to American colleges bemoaning, *"How can I compete? I didn't almost die in a Gobi Desert sandstorm. But my mom married her cleaning lady and my dad hooked up with his shrink. That's gotta count for something."* As you know, these boys have no filter, often blurting what matters most to them.

I'd expected to meet Alice at the hospital, but when I called her cell phone she was at home to take a hot shower, having spent the night in Room 413 with her mom who lay in bed beside you, her sister Heather, and your sister Elizabeth, who took turns folding themselves into uncomfortable hospital chairs, or bunking on the floor wrapped in sleeping bags they brought from home.

You're now on a morphine pump and oxygen as you've turned resolutely inward and are working at your final exit, stage right, with complete concentration. I convinced Alice to drop by the hospital *en route* to Guelph, and she cheerfully spent a moment alone with you, saying goodbye. Again.

You must be so proud of Alice. She began unraveling her tale of belief throughout our drive. How the cab driver who took her to the hospital last night told her that he was only 14 when his mom died of a brain aneurysm and that Alice needed to face your certain death and her continuing life with boldness. *"Be bold,"* he implored. I reminded her of the line from Tennessee Williams' *A Streetcar Named Desire* where Blanche Dubois admits, *"I can always depend on the kindness of strangers."* A sentiment that Alice now knows to be true.

She also believes that her mono in October was a gift to get her home to be with you before you were hospitalized this final time. She began mourning the loss of you months ago, so when her friends at university ask her how she is and she replies, *"I'm really good,"* she means it. Yes, it is awful what has happened to you and to your family as you've all faced the new normal of brain cancer, but the pain and indignity you have suffered in the past month have been too much, even for one who approached his life with hyperbole. The exaggeration is too gross this time when it matters most.

Alice hopes only for your release now. She tells me that you are planning to leave your body to the Anatomy department at the University of Toronto, if they'll take it, but she thinks that the only parts of you that haven't been contaminated by treatment for glioblastoma are your eyes, paradoxically fiery and pale as ice.

We run into snow squalls leaving Guelph and arrive back at Trillium to discover you received last rites at 2:40 p.m. Heather keeps wetting a washcloth, placing it tenderly on your head to try to cool your fever, to ease your way. Deb is on the phone with the Trillium Gift of Life fielding bizarre questions like have you been bitten by a dog? Well, yes, according to your sister Elizabeth, a white West Highland Terrier when you were a little boy. What about a squirrel? A bat?

You are working hard at moving on. When your eyebrows furrow or your limbs twitch, the person closest to the morphine pump hits the button. Your body is starting to shut down. Your hands are cold, pallid, curling in like claws. Earlier this afternoon, Deb removed your gold wedding band, twisting it round and round your ring finger, because one of the nurses remarked that someone may not be available to cut it off later. A practicality.

I wait at the hospital to drive your neighbor Iris home, because she has come to say goodbye, and until your friend Peter arrives, having flown back from business in Beijing yesterday. Heather's godmother Pat B. is also here, reminding us how she taught you to drive a stick shift, jerking and sputtering through Prince Edward County before you and Deb rented a car in the south of France in your exclusive couple time before Alice and Heather were born. Heather chimes in how you playfully warped the *"ma belle"* her grade school teacher called her into *"ma petite poubelle,"* my little garbage can, and the nickname stuck.

With Peter's arrival, I kiss Deb on both tear-wet cheeks and ask her to call me anytime over the next several hours if she wants me to come back to keep you all company.

Wednesday November 28

I dozed fitfully all night, expecting Deb to phone and tell me that you had died, but you are remarkably still here on this side, though your breathing is increasingly labored. You've transitioned to Cheyne-Stoking—a sure sign of death's dominion over life even though Dylan Thomas insisted *death shall have no dominion* and a condition I remember from bearing witness to my grandmother's last living moment as I watched her breathing pause and lengthen, then stop, as she readied herself for her final ride to her plot she would share with my grandfather in Mount Pleasant Cemetery here in Toronto.

Your sister Elizabeth decides to stay in your hospital room while I drive Deb and the girls home for showers, naps, and some fortifying French onion soup. Shortly after we arrive at the house, Pat B. calls to say that they have found you a private room where you will be moved in the next few minutes. Before we left this morning, one of the pastoral care workers dropped by to see you and commented that you are weaker and weaker, *"progressing nicely."* That your passing will not be long now. Why do they insist on using euphemisms?

Ginny calls the house from New Zealand, and Deb chatters to her only sister about the night you've all spent together where she claimed to be *"the only one awake at the Garden of Gethsemane."*

On our way back to the hospital close to three o'clock we stop at Etobicoke School of the Arts, where Heather submits her application for the theatre arts program there next Fall. It is her way of trying to establish a continuing bond with you beyond your death. She came down the stairs earlier, bouncing into the living room to have you rehearse her audition pieces with her. Her face crumpling as she slumped to the sofa then remembering where you were.

Elizabeth's husband has come to drive her home, since she is beyond exhausted. She kisses you on your forehead, whispering your childhood nickname before she leaves: *"Goodbye, Chip."*

Two church friends from All Saints Kingsway, Lori and Donna, have come by your room. Lori's on food duty and is figuring out what to bring to keep Deb, Alice and Heather fueled through their watch. Donna kept a vigil last night with all of you and is a reassuring presence, especially to Deb, since she kept a similar vigil with her own husband as he died in their home only a few years ago. You offered the "Prayers of the People" with Heather at his memorial service. Father D. put in a random guest appearance after midnight and mostly snored in the hardback chair at the foot of your bed, according to Heather, cutting a comic clownish figure with his cartoon coif, and mumbling nonsense, which your daughters found baffling, but also amusing.

Deb is at the head of your bed, curled around you, stroking your face and talking to you, imploring you to *be a good lad, Richard, and let go. It's time to let go. You've struggled enough. Move on. We'll be OK."* Alice is sitting at your side holding your curled left hand, her moccasinned feet propped on your bedrail and Heather is perched on the foot of your bed, rubbing your bare feet. Attempting to amuse you I chatter about Marlon Brando as gambler Sky Masterson in the film version of your favorite musical. How he was so deliciously sexy and considered such hot property in those days following his turn as bad boy Stanley Kowalski in *A Streetcar Named Desire,* long before his heart was tattooed with sorrow from burying his son and he ballooned to his impressive girth in *Apocalypse Now, The Godfather* and *Don Juan DeMarco.*

We are both *On the Waterfront* hot Brando enthusiasts. I am trying to goad Heather into singing some of the tunes from *Guys and Dolls,* like *"Take Back your Mink"* or *"If I Were a Bell,"* but she refuses, claiming her throat is still sore. So, I launch into my rather tepid rendition of the chorus from *"Luck Be a Lady Tonight,"* the piece that Sky Masterson croons at the underground crap game, hoping that the rhythm will spirit Heather along into joining:

Luck, be a lady tonight
Luck, be a lady tonight
Luck, if you've ever been a lady to begin with
Luck, be a lady tonight

That Frank Loesser ditty pushes you over the edge and I watch as you fly out of your crippled body and blanch chalky white and black at your fingertips in minutes. As you soar, you cry a single tear that trickles down your cheek turned closest to Deb.

Very Greta Garbo of you, Richard. You leave this earthly life at 16:54, embraced by the women who have loved you best who are sobbing with relief at your final exit.

Out of duty to you and to Deb and the girls, in the corridor I find the hospital chaplain, familiar to Heather at Kingsway College School, and she comes in to bless your body, a lovely warm-hearted, respectful gesture. When she finishes, she asks me to read aloud Psalm 23, the King James version. That is just about my undoing, but I talk myself down through the lilting rhythm of the language and hearing the trebles, in my mind's eye, sing the descant of the final lines in the Goodall version you know so well from all your years singing in church choirs:

The Lord is my Shepherd, I shall not want
He maketh me to lie down in green pastures
He leadeth me beside still waters.

. . .

Yea, though I walk through the valley of the shadow of death, I will fear
no evil: for thou art with me; thy rod and thy staff they comfort me.

. . .

Surely goodness and mercy shall follow me all the days of my life: and
I will dwell in the house of the LORD for ever.

You are gone forever. For ever.

We stay with you as your body cools, your friend Donna tucking you in as you would have tucked Alice and Heather in thousands of times as children, with the covers neatly folded under your hands. She gently checks remaining areas of warmth and puts Deb's hand behind your heart, the last place to drain of life, that pumping furnace.

One of the young nurses you admire comes in to prepare your eyes for the gift of life tissue bank, applying balm and securing them closed with damp white gauze.

Deb has asked both Peter and me to speak at the memorial service, Peter covering your young adult capers at Trinity College and me addressing your love of literature and the theatre as colleagues and friends for the past decade. Our fingers are crossed that the University of Toronto will be able to take your remains, as you'd intended. Your final wish. A parting gift.

Thursday November 29

I've met with Deb at the house to help her organize the memorial service and found a couple of poems to be read as she'd asked. Leonard Cohen's "Anthem" will be a companion piece to W.H. Auden's "Funeral Blues." It is the refrain that is so resonant since you kept your eyes resolutely on the light:

> Ring the bells that still can ring
> Forget your perfect offering
> There is a crack, a crack in everything
> That's how the light gets in.

Father T. was there as well, the retired Anglican priest, to whom you felt closest, and whom you assured of your faith in the next life, *nearer than your head is to the pillow*, as the divine Noël Coward wrote. Now that we know that your remains have been accepted by the Anatomy Department (which has me thinking of Vincent Lam's story "Take All of Murphy" and how you, too, will be an unnamed cadaver putting medical hopefuls through their paces), Father Tim can focus on the liturgical elements of the memorial service that will be held next Wednesday afternoon at St. James Cathedral, giving Ginny plenty of time to travel from New Zealand.

Heather has decided that the floral arrangement in the cathedral must include birds of paradise, orchids, tulips and irises, all plentiful in your garden when it's in bloom. She would like to say the "Prayers of the People" during the service with your friend Donna and Alice is working on a DVD to play at the reception. Alice also wants to include lyrics from a song by Xavier Rudd called *"Green Spandex"* in the bulletin. They are words that speak to her about your relationship. And, apparently she has a photo of you tucked safely away wearing navy spandex cycling shorts, your white helmet and those oversized and never fashionable 1970s shades.

Deb and the girls have agreed that the photo they will include on the front of the bulletin is of a forty-something you, crouched at one of the herb beds behind Sunset House, wearing the cerulean blue shirt that matches your eyes, snipping handfuls of fresh basil for that summer evening's bountiful meal.

Months ago you charged Giles and Doug with the responsibility for the music and they have decided to include three well-known hymns that the congregation will know and sing with full-throated enthusiasm: *King of Love, O Christ we crown Thee*; *Dear Lord and Father of Mankind;* and *The Day Thou Gavest* as well as two anthems: William Croft's *Burial Sentences* and S.S. Wesley's *Thou Will Keep Him in Perfect Peace.* The school choir will perform, though your counter-tenor warbling will be missed. Our former student, nascent opera darling and soon-to-be-proud-father-of-two Rob G. is in Toronto now, having sung the lead in *The Marriage of*

Figaro earlier this Fall and he will participate as well, the idea of which elicits tears of joy from your closest friends.

All of us are doing our best to make sure you move on in style with your hand in the direction from afar.

Ever your friend,
Janet

All the world's a stage
And all the men and women merely players:
They have their exits and their entrances;
And one man in his time plays many parts.

—William Shakespeare, *As You Like It*

EPILOGUE

Deb, Alice and Heather Holdsworth hosted a visitation before the memorial service to honor Richard's life on Wednesday December 5th, 2007. Hundreds of current and former students as well as some of their parents crowded into the stalls and spilled out into the aisles at Toronto's St. James Cathedral in the company of Richard's colleagues and friends.

It was a bright afternoon, yet through the rose window, before the service began, a rainbow appeared. It hadn't been raining. Not to be outshone by the bursting floral glory of the peonies, orchids and roses perfuming the cathedral in his memory, I figure that rainbow was Richard, embracing the colored light, twirling and swirling, illuminating the way.

In the fifteen years that have passed since Richard's death, I've often thought of the joy he would have gotten from musicals he didn't live long enough to know. How he would have been an early enthusiast for Lin-Manuel Miranda's genre-bending, explosive *Hamilton* and laughed himself silly in the stalls at the irreverent wit and genuine heart of *The Book of Mormon*. How he would have delighted in Daniel Radcliffe's ebullient, athletic, energizing song-and-dance performance as Finch in

How to Succeed in Business Without Really Trying, especially in the showstopping number "Brotherhood of Man" that the cast performed at the 2012 Tony Awards.

When I'm out walking my labs Garp and Martha along our city's beaches, creeks, and ravines, I wonder if I might someday spy Richard's blue eyes in a stranger's face. I'll never stop looking.

I miss him every day.

It only grows.

AUTHOR'S NOTE

All of the names of the students have been changed. I have referred to them by their family names, since that is the standard in a school for boys, between staff and students, but also amongst the boys themselves. There could be several Owens in a room, but it's unlikely that any of them would acknowledge being called upon. However, if you even mumble Holtby, you'll get a response.

Though teenagers then, most of them are now in their thirties, some with young families of their own.

Those who remember being in my literature classes or in Richard's plays will recognize themselves. I remain grateful for their amusing company.

APPENDIX

Authors Referenced

Margaret Atwood

W.H. Auden

Charles Baudelaire

Samuel Beckett

Alan Bennett

Dennis Bock

Pearl Buck

Barry Callaghan

Morley Callaghan

Wayson Choy

Leonard Cohen

Noël Coward

Susan Coyne

Michael Cunningham

Charles Dickens

Anne Enright

T.S. Eliot

Timothy Findley

Scott Fitzgerald

Alison Gordon

Scott Griffin

Jim Harrison

Elizabeth Hay

Ernest Hemingway

John Irving

Kazuo Ishiguro

Lloyd Jones

James Joyce

Robert Kaplow

Thomas King

Vincent Lam

Guy de Maupassant

Alexander McCall Smith

Ian McEwan

William Shakespeare

George Bernard Shaw

Elizabeth Smart

Sophocles

Wole Soyinka

Gertrude Stein

Susan Vreeland
Oscar Wilde
Tennessee Williams
William Carlos Williams

Michael Winter
Virginia Woolf
David Young

Actors, Films and Television Shows Referenced

A Beautiful Mind
Rowan Atkinson
Amarcord
Apocalypse Now
Ingmar Bergman
Blades of Glory
Marlon Brando
The Cameraman
Alannah Campbell
Dame Judi Dench
Catherine Deneuve
Marlene Dietrich
Don Juan Demarco
The Gabor Sisters
Greta Garbo
The Godfather
Guys and Dolls
Buster Keaton
Sophia Loren
The Marriage of Figaro
Mary Poppins

Mask
The Meaning of Life
Lin-Manuel Miranda
Mister Rogers Neighborhood
My Favorite Year
My Left Foot
Sir Laurence Olivier
One Flew Over the Cuckoo's Nest
Peter O'Toole
Daniel Radcliffe
Richard III
Mickey Rooney and Judy
    Garland
Frank Sinatra
Slings & Arrows
Spaceballs
Star Trek: The Next Generation
The Spy Who Shagged Me
Truly, Madly, Deeply
The Wizard of Oz

Musicals and Plays Referenced

The 25th Annual Putnam County Spelling Bee
A Midsummer Night's Dream
A Funny Thing Happened on the Way to the Forum
Anything Goes
Avenue Q
Benevolence
Burlap Bags
Bye Bye Birdie
Cabaret
Guys and Dolls
Gypsy
Hamilton
Hamlet
High Society
How to Succeed in Business Without Really Trying
Julius Caesar
Macbeth
Never Look Back
Oklahoma!
Spamalot
The Book of Mormon
The Importance of Being Earnest
The Producers
The Sound of Music
The York Cycle

ACKNOWLEDGMENTS

Thank you to my agent Philip Turner for finding a home for *How Midsummer Night* with Open Road Media and to Mara Anastas for acquiring it.

Thank you to my sister, Denise, who choreographed musicals for Richard, with untrained but enthusiastic dancers, and remembers what fun it all was.

Thank you to Ellen Barkin, who told me she believed in these words when I needed to hear it.

Thank you to John Birkett, Martha Brooks, Shivaun Hearne, Tim Hutton, Doug Jamieson, Pat Keresteci, David Kunashko, Florence Minz, Carla Palmer and Rex Pickett for their abiding friendship.

Thank you to all of the boys—now grownups with lives of their own—who spent their formative years with me in dozens of literature classes. My, you were yar.

ABOUT THE AUTHOR

Janet Somerville taught literature for twenty years. Her book about pioneering war correspondent Martha Gellhorn, *Yours, for Probably Always*, was a Book of the Day for the *Guardian* and named by *Quill & Quire* as one of the best books of 2019.

Somerville lives in Toronto, contributes frequently to the *Toronto Star* book pages, and interviews authors on stage. She can be reached at www.janetsomervillewriter.com and on Twitter @janetsomerville.

OPEN **ROAD**

INTEGRATED MEDIA

Find a full list of our authors and
titles at www.openroadmedia.com

FOLLOW US
@OpenRoadMedia